BECOMING ONE OF THE GRATEFUL DEAD

WHERE THERE'S A WILL, THERE'S A WAY

Books by Carol Weisman, MSW, CSP

- *Planned Giving Basics, The Why, The Who and The How*

- *Raising Charitable Children*

- *Transforming Ordinary People into Fundraising Superheroes ... Even Those Who Hate to Ask*

- *Losing your Executive Director Without Losing Your Way,* Carol Weisman and Richard Goldbaum

- *The Business Professional's Guide to Nonprofit Board Service,* Charles F. Damback, Oliver Tessier and Carol Weisman

- *Secrets of Successful Retreats: The Best from the Nonprofit Pros*

- *Secrets of Successful Fundraising: The Best from the Nonprofit Pros*

- *Secrets of Successful Boards: The Best from the Nonprofit Pros*

- *Build a Better Board in 30 Days*

- *A Corporate Employee's Guide to Nonprofit Board Service*

BECOMING ONE OF THE GRATEFUL DEAD

WHERE THERE'S A WILL,
THERE'S A WAY

CAROL WEISMAN MSW, CSP

F. E. Robbins
& Sons Press

SAINT LOUIS, MISSOURI

To my three amazing, brilliant, athletic and loquatious grandsons:

Frank Edward Robbins VI, aka Freddy

Thompson Barlow Robbins, aka Tommy

Elijah Ryder Robbins, aka Eli

ISBN: 978-0-9992332-1-4
Cover and interior design: n-kcreative.com
Printed in the United States of America
Published by:

 F.E.Robbins
& Sons Press

St. Louis, MO • BoardBuilders.com • carol@boardbuilders.com

Contents

Preface 1

The Seventh Child
Sam's Story 3

Beta Test Now, Endow Later
Pam Vaccaro 10

Sweet Lovin' or Paperwork
Michael McMurtrey 18

Small Estate, Big Impact
Liz and Betsy 24

When a Will Is Like Scheduling a Colonoscopy
Kenny Sigler 32

Give Now to See Your Dream Fulfilled
Lois Williams 41

To Aspire to Inspire Before He Expires
Jerry Horwitz 48

The Evolution of a Philanthropist
Lindsay Matoush 57

Sudden Wealth and Charitable Giving
Phil & Sharon Jenkins 69

Leaving More than Money
Susan J. Ellis 77

The Poet and the Planner Give It All Away
Tom Ahern & Simone Joyeaux 87

From Heartbreak to Healing
Jack Stapleton 97

"Too Bad, So Sad, Be On Time"
Carol Weisman 105

Giving Questionnaire 116
Acknowledgments 120

Preface

I was fortunate to have parents who modeled giving.

They gave to family members who were in in need and, as physicians specializing in ob-gyn, they provided free medical care to patients with financial problems. Another group they never charged for office visits were nuns. During World War II, my German Lutheran mother had just finished medical school when she became active with the anti-Nazi underground. In political hot water, she found safety with the Sisters of St. Vincent de Paul. I am not sure how long the nuns kept her in hiding, but my mother somehow managed to arrange dates during this period and the Sisters waited up at night to hear about her romantic escapades. My mother's time with these amazing women was literally lifesaving. She never forgot their courage or their kindness.

Like my parents, I offer time and money to nonprofits and financial support to family members in need. I, too, give free medical advice, although, unlike my parents, I did not take the time to go to medical school.

When I left home, I discovered that people espoused very different philosophies of giving than my parents had. From my 45 years working in the nonprofit field, I have heard many of these philosophies. Some saddened me; some surprised me; some inspired me. The stories of inspiration are the ones that compelled me to write this book.

In these pages you will meet people willing to reveal a behind-the-scenes look at their final legacies—what they are and why and how they created them. Their interviews showed courage. After all, they were confiding their thoughts and actions on two subjects often still considered taboo in our culture: Money and Death.

My hope is that their stories and lessons learned help you with your own estate decision-making journey. My greatest joy in writing this book was when an editor or advance reader said, "I never thought of that. What a great idea."

My hope is that similar light bulbs of insight illuminate your path forward.

These boots are made for giving.

— 1 —

The Seventh Child
Sam's Story

He wore a large hat. Not being from Texas, I cannot say the exact number of gallons, but a lot of gallons were involved. There is an expression in Texas: "Big hat, no cattle," meaning that the look was all smoke and mirrors. I thought he might really have cattle. I'll call him Sam.*

I was facilitating a nonprofit retreat in Houston. During the post-retreat dinner, I was fortunate enough to sit next to him. Sam had on the most amazing boots. They sort of matched the wrinkles on his face, deeply lined from too much time in the sun and probably zero awareness of sunscreen. He told me he was 83. I told him that I liked his boots.

"I shot the ol' gator myself," he said. "He was so big, I had a purse made for my wife from the same beast. After my wife died, my daughters fought over that purse."

"Why did you have to shoot your footwear? Don't they have Payless in Texas?"

He roared and slapped me on the back, causing me to come frighteningly close to doing a swan dive into the soup.

"What business are you in?" I asked after I recovered.

"Awl," which turned out to be Texan for "oil." I was wrong about the livestock. He owned plenty of cattle.

At one time he must have been about 6'3" or 6'4", but the shape of his back was beginning to resemble a question mark. He retained his barrel chest, which sported an enormous bolo tie, decorated with a piece of turquoise the size of a saucer. I thought to myself that if I had a piece of jewelry that big I'd be bent over as well.

He was a character. But what has stayed with me after meeting him years ago are his words, now imprinted on my brain. Our conversation went something like this:

"Do you mind me asking if you've left gifts to nonprofits in your estate?"

"I don't mind your asking," he said. "Yes, I have. I have six children, and I decided to divide my estate by seven. The seventh portion is for a child or children who do not have someone to care about them or love them."

"How did you set it up?"

"All six kids must agree on how to distribute the seventh portion. They don't always agree on things. In fact, they usually don't agree on things.

"Imagine that!"

"I think one of my daughters-in-law might even be a Democrat!"

"Oh my!"

"The seventh child will be getting in the healthy seven to eight figures. So the kids can divvy up the money any number of ways. They can give it to one child or several, to one specific organization or to numerous nonprofits. The rub is that they must agree. And until they agree on how to spend the money for the seventh child, no one gets a dime.

"You sound like a bit of a control freak but one who covers your bases. I admire that."

Sam laughed. "I admit it. I'm a total control junkie. Yelling at my children when they were only two was clearly a losing game. By their teen years, I was unbelievably adrift. It turns out you can't fire your kids. Thank the Lord for my sensible and understanding wife.

"How did you come up with the concept of the seventh child?"

"I decided that after my death I wanted three things for my children. I wanted them to agree on something. I wanted them to have a meaningful conversation about philanthropy, to know that they were responsible for more than their own happiness. And I wanted them to remember that I'd been a seventh child who'd grown up in an orphanage. Without the kindness and generosity of others, who gave me friendship, scholarships, advice and a helping hand, there would be no money to divide."

His face took on an odd expression.

"You look sad," I said.

"We had so little in that orphanage, and yet we shared. I gave my children so much, and yet I failed to teach them the basic concept of taking care of one another. I'm afraid I pitted them against one another, and we are all suffering from my approach to parenting. Their mother tried her best to persuade me to be less harsh, but I didn't listen. It is my one true regret. I've done a video apologizing to my kids for my poor parenting. It's VHS. Do you think that's a problem?

"I have no idea. But I can find out from my tech guy and let you know."

"Damn it, it's not over until it's over. Sharing is an important lesson no matter when they learn it."

With that, he went outside to smoke a cigar.

I was inspired by Sam's story about making efforts to right what he considered his bad parenting. When I shared his story with others, however, they responded very differently.

Estate planning attorney Larry Katzenstein said it was an interesting case. He wondered if Sam's children understood that if they gave the money to a nonprofit, the tax consequences would be quite different than if they gave it outright to a single child. A gift to a nonprofit meant the heirs couldn't identify a specific child, but the gift would significantly decrease their tax load. "Sam's children need a smart estate-planning expert involved in the process," Larry said. "The kids might not care about the tax implications, but these tax consequences can make a world of difference."

A colleague said that she would rather walk away from any amount of money than have a parent try to control her from the grave. She had a bitter, unpleasant father who'd been a POW in the Korean conflict. Because of this experience the family cut him a lot of slack. But continual derogatory comments to his daughter traumatized her. One example: "It's a good thing Gary asked you to the prom before he saw you in that dress. You look like a cow. I can only think of one reason he asked you." My friend said that the sanest move in her life was to get out from under her father's roof and influence. They have not spoken in more than a decade, and she said it's been the happiest time of her life.

A therapist friend noted that while Sam had created a video to apologize, it was to be shown *after* his death. "He could do something while still alive to form a closer bond with his children and to bring the six of them closer together," she said. "Even if they were scattered all over the world, he could clearly afford to bring them together as a family." It could be a simple weekend gathering at a neutral location they would all enjoy, such as a ski resort, Disneyland or their hometown. She advocated creating new traditions and suggested a dry run for giving away his money. This dry run could work with Sam in or out of the room but, echoing Larry's comment, would include an expert in dealing with the transition of family wealth.

And finally, a writer friend was inspired by Sam's story to change her will. Comfortable but not wealthy, she had divided her assets equally between her two sons. Because they aren't in lucrative professions, it never occurred to her to leave money to anyone but them. Hearing Sam's story, she decided to earmark a small amount to a nonprofit of their choice, so that her legacy to them would include a reminder to move through life with an awareness of those less fortunate.

Lessons learned

For the nonprofit board member or professional: Tune into the emotional undercurrents that come with gifts. Although you may not be a trained therapist (or bartender or hair stylist who often function as therapists), you might witness the giving experience as wonderful for the donor and the family or as something horrific when more money goes to a charity than to the children. You can intervene if you choose but consult others before making suggestions. One of the most difficult decisions facing wealthy parents is how much to leave their kids. Bill Gates and Warren Buffett, for example, have left their vast estates to their foundations. They want their children to experience the joy of work and achievement on their own. The children will receive enough to be comfortable but not enough to live off their inheritances. When you discuss planned giving with your donors, consider asking them what they'd like to leave their children besides money.

For donors: Whenever possible, resolve family matters in your lifetime. For many people, money symbolizes love: *The more you give me, the more you love me.* This is especially true for parents who were absent, whether because of work, divorce or illness. What a child wants is our time and attention. When the childhood ship has sailed, what a scarred adult might want is financial compensation for real or perceived slights.

Sometimes talking to a stranger is easier than talking to a friend, colleague or family member. Sam told me that I was the only person other than his attorney who knew about this aspect of his estate plan. If you are that stranger, listen carefully and consider whether to share advice.

Postscript: After the retreat where I met Sam, he shared his estate plans with the nonprofit's executive director. She encouraged him to give reconciliation a try. Though getting his family in the same room might be more difficult than achieving peace in the Middle East, Sam said that he would work on it.

To protect his privacy, Sam did not want his real name used.

Pam Vaccaro author of *Beyond the Ice Cream Cone: The whole scoop on the food at the 1904 World's Fair.*

– 2 –

Beta Test Now, Endow Later
Pam Vaccaro

Growing up, Pam Vaccaro played a game with her Aunt Marty that one day would change her life.

It was the 1950s. On an RCA black-and-white TV with a rabbit-ear antenna, Pam and her aunt watched a show called "The Millionaire." Each week from 1955-1960, a mysterious, unseen benefactor would give an ordinary person one million dollars.

Aunt Marty devised her own version of the show, where she would play the role of the millionaire and, using a real check from a defunct bank, write a check for a million dollars. Pam played the role of the executive secretary; whose job was to deliver the check to its intended recipient.

"Check in hand, I would traipse off to the foyer and knock on my uncle's office door, pretending that it was the front door where the recipients lived," said Pam. "My uncle was at work, so I'd sit in his chair and talk to the imaginary recipients across the desk. Meanwhile, Aunt Marty went off to the basement to throw in a load of laundry or to the kitchen to start dinner. When we reconvened, I told her how the money had changed the life of the family who received it.

"Once, I created a story about a woman with ten kids who got to take all of them to the toy store. Another time, the story was about a family whose house had burned down—the clothes, the food, the toys, all gone. The million dollars would make them whole again."

Despite her middle-class roots, Pam, at age seven, had already learned how much fun it can be to give to others. She also knew that money would not solve all problems, but it sure could help.

I met Pam in 1994 through our professional organization, the National Speakers Association. When I heard Pam speak, she spoke with confidence and warmth and was clearly an expert on her topic, which that day was time management. One to one, she didn't have the braggadocio that some speakers have. I immediately thought, "I want this woman as a friend and mentor." I knew that when I grew up, I wanted to speak as well and be as warm to the new speakers. (I was 45 at the time.) She was already one of the big dogs while I was a lowly puppy.

Because we were both road warriors, we seldom saw each other. But when we did it was always memorable, such as the day I ran into her at the mall.

"What are you looking for?" I asked her.

"A Secret Santa gift."

"Don't you have only one employee … your son?"

Pam cocked her head. "Yes, and what's your point? You put names in a hat and if you get your own name, you do it over."

I still laugh about it. Traditions need to be respected. I have a feeling that if Pam were in a jail cell, she would do the same thing and include the guards. No one gets left out in Pam World. Our conversation has stuck with me for years.

One day we managed to squeeze in a lunch, and Pam mentioned that she wanted to start her own foundation. Having built a successful career as a professional speaker, trainer, coach and author, it seemed the next logical step.

"Do you have around $25 million?" I asked her.

She choked on her chopped salad. "It'd be a few dollars less."

"Then I'd suggest a donor advised fund—a mini-foundation."

She looked intrigued.

I continued, "What triggered your desire to start a foundation?"

"After a long plane ride recently, I developed blood clots, and I knew I couldn't die yet. My basement is full of stuff I have to get rid of, plus I have a few other things I need to accomplish … like setting up a charitable fund."

"What do you value?" I asked her.

Pam didn't hesitate. "Kindness, compassion and the elimination of the glass ceiling for women. I want to do something special for a high school girl who exhibits kindness and consideration, because I want girls with these traits to flourish and be recognized. I've seen that the smartest, the prettiest and the most athletic always get kudos, but true kindness is rarely rewarded."

She had already discussed the idea with her high school friend Elaine, a development director at an all-girls Catholic high school, where Pam had been giving a yearly unrestricted contribution.

"Now I want to create a specific award for a girl who exemplifies kindness and compassion," Pam said. "Elaine cried when I told her. I was touched. I knew I was onto something. Elaine showed me a long list of her school's awards, most of which were for academics and athletics. Though some were for community service, not one was for kindness or compassion.

"I want it given to a senior," Pam went on, "so that the award carries the same stature as the other end-of-the-year accolades. And I want a relationship with the girl, someone I can take out to dinner, stay in touch with and help in non-monetary ways. I envision the award as a catalyst to promote a culture of kindness and compassion throughout the school.

"But at this stage, Carol, I don't know how to make it happen."

And so we began.

After listening to Pam outline her desires, we came up with the idea of starting a fund to endow an annual educational award of $1,500 to a high school girl, nominated by her classmates or teachers for exhibiting kindness and compassion. An advisory board that she'd appoint would review the nominations.

Pam chose the school where she and her friend Elaine attended: Notre Dame High School in St. Louis. They were one of the few all-girls school that offered individualized learning as far back as the 1970's.

Step two was deciding how she wanted the money spent.

"Do you want to consider education in the broadest of terms?" I asked. "Meaning the award can be spent on travel, volunteer work, mission trips … ballet, cello or martial arts lessons … leadership workshops … self-improvement programs … and, of course, college."

"Yes!" she said. "Great idea!" She wanted the award to extend a warm arm, not limit in a boa constrictor-hold.

Pam also decided that each recipient would be asked to give away 10% of the award. This tithe could be for a friend or relative in need, her school, place of worship, or any other nonprofit. As we discussed all the possibilities, Pam's excitement was so palpable I got goosebumps.

Next, I suggested that she herself give out the award. After all, she is a professional speaker. When Pam emitted an excited squeal, we began crafting her speech.

She decided that a dry run in her lifetime would give her a chance to tweak the process and ascertain its value to recipients. The inaugural gift will be awarded in May 2019.

The advisory board will include two close friends, Pam's son and a cousin. "They know my heart, so if it stops beating, I know they'll continue the award."

Finally, we talked about how to fund this award if it were a major success. To endow it in her will would cost about $300,000, assuming a 5% interest rate. To fund it for 20 years at $1,500 a year would cost $30,000. After 20 years, a past recipient, another donor, one of her two sons or members of the advisory board could continue funding the scholarship. Pam would meet with her financial planner to devise a strategy that best aligns with her finances.

By the end of lunch, we'd set up Pam's mini-foundation. The reason we could do it so easily: Pam came with a clear philosophy of giving, beginning with Aunt Marty and her "Millionaire" game.

Another influence was *The Sacred Heart of the World*, a book by David Richo.

"It wasn't the type I normally pick up, but its basic message touched me: How can I best love in this lifetime? How do I make life easier for others who share this planet? I had assumed that I'd read a few pages and then toss it in a Goodwill bin. I was wrong. Its message of kindness and compassion changed my life.

"I entered a religious order at 18 but after six years, struggling with celibacy, I left the convent and haven't belonged to a church since. When my dad came down with Alzheimer's, I became his advocate in the nursing home. That's when I became more spiritual. Kindness and compassion trump all the do's and don'ts of Catholicism.

"During this time, I decided to write a thank-you note each week to surprise someone who'd made my life better. With this decision, I began to see gratitude everywhere."

Pam thanked the woman who grew tulips at the top of their street, as well as the staff at her local McDonalds.

When a roofing company fixed the leak on her house, she thanked them for making her life easier and drier. She thanked a turkey company for their clear directions on cooking, and they sent her a turkey. "That was a surprise!" she said. Pam also wrote a note to a 19-year-old boy who had fixed her car. "Much to my surprise, he wrote back: 'When I read your thank-you note, it felt like I'd gotten a million dollars. (Thank you, Aunt Marty!) And my boss gave me a promotion.'

"One doesn't expect to get a thank-you note for a thank-you note," said Pam. "I wondered if I should write a thank-you note for the thank-you note for the thank-you note. Then I said to myself, 'Pam, get a grip.'"

Ten years later, Pam is still writing notes. It's part of the Millionaire Story—surprising someone with an act of kindness.

Unsurprisingly, kindness runs in her genes. When Pam's mother was in high school, she won a Miss Kindness pin, which Pam safeguards with her mother's wedding ring and other keepsakes.

"That award still has meaning today, still resonates. I fantasize about the recipient of my award telling her teenage daughter about it one day. I'm excited to fine-tune the details of my fund. Hopefully, I'll live long enough to personally know and help the first recipients. To think that what I'm creating with this fund could last decades is an astonishing thought."

Lessons learned

For donors: Creating a plan to give after your demise doesn't need to take months or years if you are clear on your philanthropic intent. You don't have to be a millionaire to make a difference. Pam chose to be very specific in her giving: a specific type of student at a specific school. She decided to beta test her plan within her lifetime. You can be as general or as specific as you want depending on your desires. For instance, you can give to a specific hospital to combat infant mortality or you can let your personal "committee" choose the hospital.

Also consider that Pam is working on a back-up plan. Schools come and go. What if the school closes, burns to the ground or brings in a new administration that doesn't value a kindness award? In the same vein, a family friend set up a fund to provide free obstetrical care to women without insurance. Months after she died, the selected hospital stopped doing obstetrics. Without a plan B, the desired fund fueled a big family quarrel.

For nonprofits: Ask your donors to put their intentions in writing and to share them with you to ensure clarity regarding your nonprofit's responsibility. Pam's friend Elaine might retire or die before the program is fully launched and enmeshed in the school's culture. Archive as much donor documentation as you can. Share with others the contribution, motivation and joy this award brings to both your donor and your organization. This recognition will encourage others to make similar gifts.

Mary and Michael McMurtrey

— 3 —

Sweet Lovin' or Paper Work
Michael McMurtrey

Michael knew something was wrong.

"I know you'll think I'm crazy," he said to his wife Mary, "but I have a feeling I'm sick. For the last couple of months, I haven't been able to eat right. I can't sleep right. At the end of a long run, I feel no endorphin release. I'm an athletic guy, and I'm pretty in tune with my body. Something's not right."

Mary nodded, half concerned, half unconvinced. He *looked* okay to her.

A few weeks later, Mary and Michael had Friday night dinner plans with friends, but Michael was in such excruciating pain that he called his doctor. "Either you have a torsion of the testicles or nothing," he said. "Worst case scenario, you are going to lose a testicle. Best case scenario, you blow a few hundred dollars on an unnecessary ER visit."

The doctor was wrong. There was a third option. And it was worse.

Michael didn't want Mary and his two daughters, ages five and eleven, to hang around an ER on a Friday night, so he drove himself to the hospital. The ER staff gave him something for the pain. In a Demerol haze, Michael realized that they were examining the left side of his body. The testicle, now grapefruit-size, was on the right.

"What's going on?" he asked the nurse. "Why are you examining the wrong side of my body?"

Before she could answer, the doctor walked in to examine him.

"What's with the black scrubs? Are you the doctor of death?" Michael asked him. "I want to talk to someone about the left side of my body. Doctor, it's my right testicle that's killing me. Can we talk about that?"

"No," said the doctor, "we aren't going to talk about that."

Why not? Michael thought but was too drugged to say aloud.

"We think we found cancer on the left side of your body," the doctor continued. "We don't know for sure."

Michael took a cab home. He was 47 years old and had to tell his wife and children that he might have cancer. He felt oddly affirmed—something *was* wrong.

He spent the weekend getting physician referrals from friends.

Monday morning, the first referral doctor said he was 99% sure it was cancer but could not say definitely until he removed the testicle.

"What else could it be?" Michael asked.

"Nothing," said the doctor.

"Why couldn't it be something else?"

"Because nothing else looks like this."

Michael's canary in the coal mine was a swollen testicle on the right, even though the cancer was on the left.

Wednesday morning, Michael saw a second urologist, who said that Michael had the fastest growing type of cancer—it can double in size every three days.

Thursday morning, Michael's surgery was scheduled.

Michael had a will he felt good about until Wednesday evening when it dawned on him: If the surgeon makes a mistake, I'm dead.

He and Mary sat down with the girls. "I want you to know that I'm sick," he said. "I am going to have an operation. And I am determined to live."

Everyone cried.

After Michael put the girls to bed, he pulled out all his financial and estate documents so that Mary would know where everything was. Michael was a wealth manager, so he was organized. As he soon discovered, however, the information was organized for him but not for anyone else. Specifically, the key to the safety deposit box was in his personal safe at home, but he was the only who knew the combination. Mary's name was on the box, but she didn't know where the key was. Because he was the money guy, she hadn't bothered learning where everything was and he hadn't bothered teaching her. Because of his extensive financial background, investments in old partnerships were scattered in several places. Michael knew where they were. He also knew that Mary would never find them. Mary didn't know his email accounts or how they were used. She didn't know the passwords. Some of his email accounts were even encrypted. Michael said, "We aren't talking illicit affairs, we're talking money." After hours of going through this stuff with Mary, it was past midnight. Michael collapsed, exhausted.

Lying in bed, he started talking to Mary. "I'm scared," he said. "I'm in pain. But I'm not afraid of dying. What I'm afraid of is leaving my daughters fatherless."

He knew the financial mess would eventually sort itself out. "It was the only time I wished I had more life insurance."

If everything had been in order, he would not have spent what was potentially his last night on earth worrying about the money. The passcodes. The email accounts. The limited partnerships. He would much rather have been having what he called "sweet lovin" with Mary than worrying about money.

Michael and Mary got up a few hours later to be on time for his surgical appointment. Michael's dad, who had been given the news beforehand, came over early to take the girls to school. He was his usual stoic, supportive self. Before the girls awakened, Michael and Mary left for the hospital not knowing what the outcome would be but secure that their daughters would be well taken care of during this long, difficult day.

In the pre-op area, the surgeon was joking about removing the wrong testicle, which Michael found incredibly not funny. He didn't need one more thing to be worried about. Michael understood that they were removing the left one, even though the pain was in the right. Michael knew that the doc was trying to lighten the mood, but he wasn't having any of it. He heard the doc say to the nurse that he was on day three of a fasting cleanse. Michael's last conscious thought was, *You had better not be light-headed.*

When Michael woke up in the recovery room his first thought was, *I'm alive.* He was apprehensive about his health but grateful that his daughters wouldn't be father-less. He hadn't worried about his resilient wife or some other man calling her "Sweetie." He was worried that his girls would call some other man "Daddy." Michael was in pain but relieved.

The doctor said that the surgery was a success and Michael could go back to work in three days, but that turned out to be dead wrong. For the next week and a half, Michael walked around doubled over. Four years later, he still feels pain in the prosthetic testicle, but he is afraid to have it removed. For now, the pain is manageable.

Michael didn't need radiation or chemo. The oncologist said that the surgery had been a silver bullet, meaning that he was 90% sure the cancer was gone. To be 100% sure he would need an additional, high-risk treatment. Michael was good with 90%.

Michael's message to his clients and friends: If you are not legally and financially organized, do so immediately. You don't want to spend what could be your last night on earth doing paperwork.

Lessons learned

For nonprofit leaders: Even your most organized donors might not have shared important information with a spouse, a child, a friend or other trusted person. Without the sharing of this information (including all those pesky passwords we are encouraged to continually change), not only do the survivors have to deal with grief but also a headache-inducing digital treasure hunt. To make life easier for the donor and the donor's family as well as for your nonprofit, you might want to share an estate planner with them. My personal favorite: youthbridge.org.

For donors: Vital information related to your estate plan can be stored in a shared safety deposit box, and both spouses should know the combination to the safe. If that's not the case, the surviving partner can have the box drilled, but who wants to pay for that and wait around at such a difficult time?

When my husband and I filled out our estate planner document, we were amazed to discover how much information we didn't know about each other, from his military records to, yes, all our individual passwords and passcodes.

Note to self: Update everything next week!

The power of shared coffee and confidences.

— 4 —

Small Estate, Big Impact
Liz and Betsy

The great-granddaughter of a slave, Liz took pride in working as a cleaning lady for a select number of clients. She also prided herself in working only for people she liked. One such person was Betsy, a full-time mother, volunteer and trust fund "child" married to an attorney.

Liz and Betsy were an unlikely pair. Betsy was 5'10" and, when not sporting jodhpurs and riding boots, wore Lily Pulitzer dresses without stockings over her long, muscular legs. Liz was 5' nothing, with a bosom extending from her collarbone to her waist and nylons rolled up over her knees. Since her first interview, every time Liz came to work, Betsy served her coffee in a porcelain cup—their morning ritual. Being served by this regal white woman amused the heck out of Liz.

After Liz had been working for Betsy for about eight months, Betsy said, "You never smile."

Liz lowered her head. "It's my teeth."

"I can't have someone working for me who doesn't smile."

Liz's heart sank. No more porcelain cup, no more great pay.

"We have to get them fixed!"

And with those words, Betsy picked up the phone and called a dentist friend who owed her a favor. Liz was dumbfounded listening to this "crazy white woman" bully the dentist into seeing Liz the next day.

"Send me the bill," Betsy said, "and it better be reasonable!"

Betsy got off the phone, wrote the dentist's name and address on a sheet of paper and briskly presented it to Liz. With all the pomp and circumstance of a regency dowager, Betsy then said, "When your teeth are perfect, I expect you to continue working for me. I don't want to see you flashing your new smile on "America's Next Top Model." At which point, both women giggled like gossipy sixth graders.

Betsy loved two things: her family and her horses. And she valued precision, as did her husband Andrew, who could be a bit OCD. So, when Liz cleaned their home, she kept her routine focused and efficient. She would put in a load of wash, clean a room, transfer the wash to the dryer, clean another room, iron while putting in the next load, then clean another room. She ironed everything in sight, including Andrew's handkerchiefs and boxer shorts. He called her "The Michelangelo of the Ironing Board." When Betsy went into the laundry room after Liz left, every piece of clothing looked like it could once again hang from the racks of Gap Kids, Saks and Brooks Brothers.

Betsy enjoyed asking Liz about her life, so Liz enjoyed talking about it. Her husband Johnny was steadily employed as a union ironworker. He didn't hit her or drink to excess. Liz thought he was a good man but mule-headed. She admitted to Betsy that her bar for a good marriage was pretty low. She took pride in the fact that they owned their home and cars and could give something every week to their church. They had one son who was a chef. Though he left home the day he graduated from high school, he and Liz talked at least once a week.

One day, Betsy sensed that something was wrong in Liz's life. "Are you okay?" she asked.

Liz confided that her son had contracted HIV and Johnny forbid her to visit him because, as her husband put it, "This is God's way of punishing the sodomite." Liz became severely depressed.

When she heard the story, Betsy said, "Johnny is not the boss of you!" She then bought a plane ticket so that Liz could visit her son on the West Coast. This was the first of many trips that Betsy and her husband Andrew financed for Liz. And when Liz's son died, her husband Johnny refused to spend one cent on a gravestone, so

Betsy and Andrew paid for that, too. A small memorial service was held at their church, which Johnny refused to attend. Betsy, Andrew, and their three young sons showed up in their Sunday best. Liz held it together until 10-year-old Andy, the oldest, said, "It doesn't seem fair to me that your son died and Johnny is still alive." Betsy almost choked. Liz laughed through her tears. She hugged Andy and assured him he was correct.

As the years passed and Johnny was diagnosed with Alzheimer's, Betsy helped Liz find a nursing home for him. And when Liz, now 70, needed a knee replacement, Betsy suggested that she stop working and start collecting Social Security.

Liz took Betsy's advice—she didn't want to work anymore—but she missed the company of her clients. She visited Johnny daily but he no longer recognized her, and soon the visits were so tiring that Liz wasn't sure she still cared whether he thought she was his wife or the Queen of England.

Every week or so, Betsy checked in with her former housecleaner and, sensing Liz's loneliness, suggested that she get a dog. Johnny had never permitted an animal in the house, so Liz, with a growing streak of mutiny, liked the idea. She recalled her orthopedic surgeon's post-operative advice: "Walk your dog daily, even if you don't have one." Liz took those words to heart.

So off Betsy and Liz went to an animal rescue organization to look for an older dog that wouldn't be too wild. After three visits, Liz adopted a tiny white ball of fur that she named Princess. Betsy wasn't in love with Princess. She didn't care that the puppy was a mutt, but

Betsy believed in big dogs like labs or boxers, at least 50 or 60 lbs. of something. Regardless, Betsy paid for the dog's shots and spaying—her retirement gift to Liz.

When Liz came to visit Betsy, with Princess in tow, the love of Liz's life bit Betsy's calf, drawing blood on her white silk pants. Betsy spluttered, "That is the world's most obnoxious dog!"

"Your boys were not always the politest or tidiest children in the world!" Liz retorted.

"Well, at least they didn't bite!"

After Johnny passed away, Liz came for a visit, bringing her trademark sweet potato pie. Over coffee and pie, Betsy asked Liz what she was going to do with her estate. Liz almost choked laughing.

"I don't exactly live in Downton Abbey."

"You may not live in a mansion," Betsy said, "but you have a choice. The government can get your house, car, insurance and savings, or *you* can decide what to do with your assets. What do you really care about?"

Liz blurted, "Princess."

Seconds later, she added, "And of course, you and Andrew and the boys."

"If you'd like, your estate can go to the animal shelter where you got Princess. I'll get one of Andrew's partners to write a simple will. I'm sure they'll do it pro bono."

"How much is pro bono?" Liz asked.

"It's fancy lawyer talk for free."

Liz let out a sigh of contentment. As she drove off that day, she was beaming.

The day of the appointment, Betsy accompanied Liz to the attorney's office and sat in the waiting room while

Liz shared her wishes with him. The attorney then asked Betsy to join them. "Would you be the executor?" he asked her.

"No. I don't want to deal with all the paperwork."

The three of them agreed that the attorney would take care of it and that his fee would come out of the estate.

The lawyer continued. "Liz is leaving you Princess."

Betsy gasped but recovered quickly. "I'm happy to ensure that she's taken care of, but I'd rather have shingles than adopt that dog."

"Shingles isn't an alternative," said the somewhat humor-impaired attorney.

After further discussion, the three decided that Betsy would find someone who would love and care for Princess just as Liz had.

Liz was happy. Betsy was happy. The attorney was happy. And, had it known at the time, the animal rescue shelter would have been happy. Depending on real estate values and the amount of funds that Liz would need at the end of her life, this nonprofit was going to receive a gift ranging between $150,000 and $200,000. And the gift would be from a donor whose name the nonprofit didn't even know.

Lessons learned

For nonprofit leaders: You will receive gifts and find that you have no record of any relationship between the donor and your organization. There is usually a link, but you might not find it. Betsy's name was on the check for the adoption, spaying and shots.

People can own significant estates even if they don't live in a Downton Abbey-esque manor. Many of us mistakenly assume that people who live in modest homes, drive late-model cars and bring gifts of sweet potato pies don't have financial resources.

If you don't want your state government to decide where your assets go and who will care for your children, pets and property, see a lawyer and get a will.

Every state is different. In Missouri, if your estate is worth more than one million dollars and goes to probate, the assigned attorney receives a minimum of $26,000. The purpose of probate is to make sure your creditors get paid. For far less than $26,000, hire an attorney and get your end-of-life affairs in order. This includes a medical power of attorney.

If you are asked to be an executor or to care for minor children or, heaven forbid, an animal that you can't abide, you can negotiate before a death if you are specifically asked to be responsible. You might live in a no-pet building. You might have a specific religious affiliation that would conflict with the requests of parents. For instance, if you go to Mass every Sunday and your friend or family member wants their children to go to a Methodist service, you might have to do some negotiating. (I am reminded of a friend's daughter telling her kindergarten class that she had a new dog, Chester. When the teacher asked what kind of dog, she answered, "Presbyterian." A cute story, but also a sign that religious beliefs may affect how children and pets are cared for.)

On a more serious note, a friend of mine thought a relative might be a pedophile and left specific instructions that her children were not to be left alone with him under any circumstances. Many years later, when her children were grown and the relative had died, her suspicions were confirmed.

When you identify what you truly care about and allocate finances to honor that passion, the decision will bring you not only joy but a sense of peace.

Kenny, Ben, Beka, and Jude Sigler

— 5 —

When Writing a Will is like Scheduling a Colonoscopy
Kenny Sigler

Normally, I wouldn't ask a colleague if he or she had a will. The question is too personal. But with Kenny I felt entitled. Not only because we were colleagues who became friends but also because at 29 he was young enough to be my grandson.

"I know that with a wife and child I need a will," he answered. "But there is so much thought and work involved."

"Which is the exact reason to get going on it now," I said. "Do you want to decide who has custody of your son, or would you rather have the state make the decision if you and Beka die at the same time? I assume you periodically drive in the same car with your wife, which is far more dangerous than flying together. But not to worry! I am sure you trust the great state of Texas to make wise decisions about your life insurance, your house, your cars and your savings."

"You know, as a kid I was up to all kinds of shenanigans that adults warned me about, like doing flips into the shallow end of the pool," Kenny countered. "Nothing ever happened."

"I assume you know that you aren't a kid anymore?"

Kenny sagged like a teenager who was told he couldn't have the car until he'd cleaned his room.

"I'll talk to Beka about it."

"Good man. I'll call you in a month to see how the will is coming along."

When I first met Kenny, he worked for Abegg Willis, a consulting firm in Tyler, Texas. He was a real Southern Boy. At the office he would not let his boss pick up anything heavier than three sheets of paper. Not because she was in her mid-70s but because Kenny had been raised to be a gentleman. He was also a quick study. Whenever I mentioned a book to him, within the week he had bought it, read it and asked questions about it. I figured he would approach getting his will done with the same gusto.

I was wrong.

It took him three weeks to summon the courage just to broach the *idea* of a will with his wife. I didn't understand his resistance. They seemed like a close and loving couple. From every conversation we'd had, it appeared they communicated well. But this topic he couldn't seem to wrap his head around. When I asked why, he seemed as baffled by his behavior as I was.

It wasn't as though the couple didn't know each other well or share the same values. They met as children when Beka's dad was Kenny's T-ball coach. Attending different schools, they didn't see much of each other growing up but reconnected years later at their church's Sunday School class for college-age congregants. "People say they see someone and just know. I just knew," said Kenny. "I liked the way she looked, smiled, moved. I knew she was the woman for me."

After a few months traveling in the same circles, the couple finally began dating. "I did things I had never done before. I bought her flowers and shoes and took her to Dallas by train. I started to wonder who I was. I was smitten." Seven months later, Kenny proposed.

His voice softens when he speaks about his wife. You can *hear* his affection and admiration.

For weeks after our conversation, Kenny would come home, rush around with Beka to get dinner on the table, give their toddler a bath and collapse into bed. Over the course of the evening they'd talk about their workdays, their families, their friends and their church. But end of life was a topic they had never discussed.

Part of not bringing up the subject of a will, said Kenny, was that he was so exhausted. Many nights he just plain forgot. Beka worked full-time as an orthopedic nurse, which meant 12-hour shifts every weekend and at least once during the week, so he was careful to safeguard her time. "I didn't know how welcoming she'd be to have this conversation. I wasn't worried that she'd react badly. It was more that she wouldn't want to take the time to think about it. It would feel like one more task she'd have to do.

"I also didn't know if I was intellectually or emotionally up to this discussion. I wasn't sure I had all the answers or even all the questions. During the day at work, I'd think I should talk to her about it that night. But at home that evening I'd wonder how I was going to bring it up.

"It all felt like a new weight, like having to get my taxes done but without a time limit.

"Finally, a bell went off. We were driving at the time, so we were trapped in the car, and I didn't have to look her in the face. I didn't want to have this conversation, so I eased into it by blaming Carol. 'Carol said we have to do this!' Beka's reaction shocked me. She sighed a deep breath of relief that we were finally going to talk about it. She had been really worried about the future but was too perplexed about how to talk about our deaths. I thought it was going to be a long and dark conversation, and it wasn't."

When it came to getting the will written, the biggest and most time-consuming challenge was choosing the right attorney. "Which one matches where we are in life? Who do we go with? We didn't want or need someone from a big firm who did big-time estates for big-time fees."

The couple's financial planner recommended Legal Zoom, an online company that offers consumers legal documents without the hassle of having to hire a lawyer. I advised against it. I had heard from too many estate-planning attorneys who claim that they owed much of their business to Legal Zoom, because folks didn't understand the implications of the legalese and the result was a mess. Also, different states have different laws. Some states require a notary to make changes. Others require two witnesses—another reason you need a lawyer who knows federal tax laws as well as the estate and tax laws in your state.

One financial advisor's example: Let's say you have an estate valued at $1 million, with your house worth half a million and an IRA valued at another half. If your daughter wants the house and your son wants the IRA, who gets the most money? If you answered the daughter, you are correct. The IRA will be taxed at nearly 30% because your not-so-favorite Uncle Sam wants his share and the money has not yet been taxed. By comparison if the daughter sells the home, she would pay only 6% for a real estate commission. If she kept it or sold it herself, she would pay no tax. These are the kinds of issues in which a specialist is well-versed.

Kenny resumed his research on attorneys. At an annual professional conference, a lawyer reached out to him, wanting to know more about the nonprofit where Kenny was the development director. The two started talking and hit it off. When Kenny discovered they had mutual friends, "I knew I'd found our attorney."

That decision took more than a year. "What's taken even longer," he said, "is answering all the questions about who gets our kids."

During this same period, the couple had another son, Ben. "With an infant and a three-year-old I knew we had to step up our timeline. We continually debated who should raise our kids if something happened to us."

At first, they thought Beka's parents would make the best guardians. They were loving and caring grandparents. But with the birth of a second child, the couple had to consider the grandparents' ages. Would they want to care for Jude and Ben—or even be able to—when they were in their 80s?

The couple next considered Beka's sister and brother-in-law, who had three kids. Raising five children is exponentially more difficult than raising three, however, and Kenny and Beka grew concerned that an extra two might be too great a burden.

Finally, the couple decided that Beka's younger sister and her husband would make the ideal guardians. They were young and childless, practiced the same faith and shared the same values. "We knew they'd take good care of them," said Kenny. "We've already talked to them about it, so we know they're comfortable with the idea. We plan to sit down with them one more time to make the official ask. They want children of their own, so if they have triplets or a child with special needs, we may have to rethink this. But for today we've made a decision we feel good about."

Kenny and Beka are now two years into working on their will. They have hired an estate-planning attorney and secured guardians for their children. They have thought through their charitable giving that will leave bequests to their church, an adoption agency (because they plan to adopt one day); Gospel for Asia, committed to spreading the Gospel throughout the continent; and their children's potential guardians.

"This journey has not been a weekend jaunt," said Kenny. "It's been more like an extended trip around the world. But we are committed to getting this completed, and soon. It's wise to plan for our family and smart to have a will.

"Plus, we know that if we don't get it done, we'll have to deal with Carol. In addition to being my friend and colleague she's our self-appointed legal dominatrix."

Lessons learned

For nonprofit leaders: It can take a long time for people to complete their estate planning. For many, discussing the possibility of their demise is difficult. Potential donor issues: If there are young children, who would be willing and able to take them for 10, 12, or 18 years? What non-profits, if any, do I want to support? (Hopefully, yours.) Although 90% of all gifts to nonprofits are simple bequests, is a simple bequest the right way to go in terms of taxes, retirement needs and other obligations? Do I want to be an organ donor? (In some states, this decision is made when you get a driver's license.) Do I want to be buried in the family plot where my first spouse is interred?

Estate planning is a complex process. You can help folks by asking if they would like you to hold them accountable. I've asked this question of a number of people, and all but one said yes. I ask when I should call them. Some say, "In a month, by which time I'll have an appointment with an attorney." If they live in my home state of Missouri, I ask if they would like a list of estate-planning attorneys in the area. I have been calling one friend regularly for a year and a half. Her excuse: She and her husband haven't had time to get it done. And they are both lawyers! I don't nag or harangue or scold. My calls are only to lend support for something important that will protect their family and legacy. I have never heard anyone say, "Oh, I'd really like my legacy to cause a major family feud that results in more attorneys purchasing bigger and better cars." No one wants to leave a mess behind for loved ones to clean up. Unfortunately, without a will that's exactly what can happen.

For donors: Set a timeline to get your estate in order, which for many means updating a current will. When a friend who was to be our executor died, my husband and I waited over a year to find a replacement. We knew we needed one, but the thought of expending time and energy on a difficult decision made it easy to procrastinate. In our case, it was also just plain negligence. And we knew it.

Nine of the individuals profiled in this book revealed in their interviews that they need to make changes to their will. The biggest excuse for not getting it done? Lack of time. The second biggest: Money. Writing, changing or updating an estate plan can sit on the back burner for years. But when the heat turns up and catastrophe strikes, you and your loved ones can get burned. By the way, I am one who needs to do some updating!

Here's my advice for us procrastinators: Think of a will like a colonoscopy. The prep may be awful, but the procedure is a piece of cake. In both cases, you need a professional to take a periodic look to ensure that everything is in order. Laws, charitable intentions, family and friends—all can change over time. Take care of yourself, your loved ones and the organizations that espouse your values, and you will make a difference in this life and the next.

Lois sharing her delight at the new educational panels
installed at Star Island, New Hampshire.

— 6 —

Give Now to See Your Dream Fulfilled
Lois Williams

Lois Williams received her first standing ovation when she was 83. Not when she earned her Ph.D. in early childhood education while raising six children. Not when she was speaking about the book she wrote at age 73 titled, *Religion on the Isles of Shoals*. She received it when she donated $300,000 to Star Island, a religious and educational retreat on 45-acre island ten miles off the coasts of New Hampshire and Maine.

Lois had long been passionate about history, and nothing fascinated her more than the history of Star Island, from its origins as a fishing village in the early 1600s to its evolution as a conference and retreat center and summer colony for the literary and artistic elite. Guests have included poet Celia Thaxter and impressionist painter Childe Hassam.

In 1975, Lois began attending conferences at Star Island with her husband Pete, a government engineer, and their six children.

Lois and Pete were not wealthy. They were middle class people who, after World War II, were smart enough to buy a home for $30,000 in Potomac, Maryland. They lived frugally, and Pete was a smart investor. Being a couple of a certain era, Lois had a household allowance. The feminist in her insisted on a separate account.

After five decades together, Pete developed dementia. Lois dreaded going to the nursing home to see her beloved husband's deterioration. To keep her mind active while caring for Pete, Lois came up with the idea of a one-page history of the island for educating children, her second passion.

As a member of the Star Island Corporation, she wanted to get on the Island History and Artifacts Committee. The corporation sent out yearly notes asking on which committee corporation members wanted to serve. Every year Lois requested History and Artifacts; every year she was assigned a committee other than the one she wanted. But Lois was tenacious. She decided to send the corporation a gift of $5,000. Lo and behold, she got on the committee she wanted.

There she met Irene Bush, a former president of the board of directors who shared Lois's interest in the history of the Isles of Shoals. Irene and her husband, a retired banking executive, were the best of both worlds: rich *and* generous. Because of Irene's life as a philanthropist, Lois respected her insights on giving. When Lois began to contemplate making a significant gift, she consulted her friend, who said it was a great idea. All systems were go.

It is noteworthy that Lois did not discuss her plans with any of her six children or their spouses, some of whom were lawyers. "I am fond of all of them," she said, "but we are private people. I don't discuss matters of consequence with them, nor do they with me. That is just how we are." Because of her husband's illness, Pete was also not involved, so the decision to give the gift was Lois's alone.

Originally, Lois was going to divide her assets in her will among her four daughters and two sons. Not one of her children is wealthy, but all are comfortable. All would have a more secure retirement if Lois adhered to her original plan. And yet, Lois decided to give $300,000 to Star Island during her lifetime so that she could see her vision for the Island come to life, so she could participate in the dream.

Lois's desire was to share Star Island's history and sustainability programs with conferees, island visitors and school children. To that end, she restricted her gift to upgrading Vaughn Cottage, which houses the Celia Thaxter Museum; renovating the building which shelters the Rutledge Marine Lab; and creating a large wall exhibit displaying the history of the Isles of Shoals.

Lois had a location in mind for the exhibit. But in working closely with Joe Watts, the Island CEO, she was persuaded that another site, on the island's main walking path, would better achieve her goals. The first initiative they tackled was the educational display. Lois gave a vague outline of what she wanted to see in the exhibit. Fast forward nine months, and the panels were unveiled. They were in color and twice the size of those in the original plans. Lois adored them.

The Vaughn Cottage renovation was another smooth undertaking. "The finished product was so much more than my original vision," Lois said. "The workmanship was outstanding. I was thrilled."

The Rutledge Marine Lab was a different story, however, because people kept making suggestions for improvements along the way. Much like getting new carpeting, one suddenly realizes that the drapes look dingy, and well, the walls could use a coat of paint and what about the lighting? The amount Lois had donated did not cover everything because the project kept expanding to include composting toilets, informational kiosks for visitors, seating for an outdoor classroom, updated equipment in the lab—an entire rehab. The whole project was well beyond Lois' means; however others were inspired to contribute.

Today, Lois is physically healthy—she walks three miles a day—and mentally sharp. There is no reason to believe that she won't live another 10 to 15 years, potentially outliving her assets. When asked why she gave during her lifetime rather than as a part of her estate plan, she said, "I wanted to play a part in the planning of the project. I wanted some control. I would not have left this gift in my will but would have simply divided my estate by six.

"Outliving my assets," she continued, "never crossed my mind"—no doubt the result of decades of living within her means.

Lois never craved recognition, so she worried about being perceived as a show-off. Instead, people continually thank her for making history accessible. The public reaction has been both a surprise and a delight.

But life can be bittersweet. Five of Lois's six children have supported her decision to give her money to the Island; one child has not. It's a subject that must be painful—Lois refused to talk about it.

An unexpected outcome of her gift: She's been given a special historic cottage for her summer visits, where she's frequently fussed over. The exhibit, while not part of her initial vision, is a continual source of joy.

"Seeing the results of my gift," she said, "has been one of the most gratifying experiences of my life."

Lessons learned

For board and staff: Lois went from being an annual donor of $1000 to a gift of $5,000 in 2015, to a gift of $300,000 in 2016. Steward all your donors like mad. You can also leverage these large acts of generosity to get more people involved both financially and intellectually, to make the project bolder and more comprehensive. Lois's generosity inspired many other individuals and grant funders. Lois lit the torch and carried it a long distance; others have since taken it forward.

In addition, be careful to limit naming opportunities to no more than 20 years. A lot of the work funded by Lois's gift will need to be redone or upgraded because of new technology (such as the new solar panels now used on the Island), weather damage and heavy use. When additional funding is needed to renovate a building, for example, you want to be free to rename it. The right of first refusal should always be given to the donor or donor's family. Stipulations need to be in writing.

For donors: If you like to be in control, give during your lifetime. It is far more difficult to achieve your philanthropic goals beyond the grave if circumstances have changed with your charity after your death. For instance, a man who lived in our neighborhood left a lot of money for research to find a cure for polio. It was a highly restricted gift made 20 years before he died in a will that was never updated. At the time of his death, the Salk vaccine was widely available. Because of the tight restrictions, his bequest was a mess to unravel.

Have a clear goal. Lois wanted to make the history of the Island a part of every visitor's experience. By partnering with the Island CEO, she could achieve far more than her original plan. The site she'd envisioned for the exhibition was moved to a location with more foot traffic. Her vision for two buildings expanded as others hopped on the Lois-fueled generosity train.

Giving a large chunk of money can have familial repercussions. Although Lois had the approval and blessing of five of her children, her decision dismayed the sixth. This still-painful reaction was the only unpleasant aspect of the gift. Whether you are a donor or a nonprofit professional, be aware that your actions might cause friction. Look to someone you trust to sign off on your idea. For Lois, that someone was her friend Irene Bush. Once Irene said it was a great idea, Lois could commit wholeheartedly.

If done properly, a gift in your lifetime can bring both excitement and joy. Others can get in on the act and make your dream bigger and better. Even if recognition is not the primary or even secondary motivation, appreciation can be more than great fun. It can be deeply gratifying.

Jerry and Bobby Horwitz volunteering at a food pantry.

— 7 —

He Aspires to Inspire Before He Expires
Jerry Horwitz

Twelve years ago, Jerry Horwitz spent $50,000 on a will.
"How on earth could it cost that much?" I asked him.

"We had a Chicago lawyer whose office was on the 63rd floor, just a few floors down from God. Such a view."

After the couple signed the will, they headed home. As Jerry got out of the car, his wife Bobbi asked him, "Where are you going?"

"Into the house," he answered.

"It isn't yours anymore," she said. "Neither is your business." And she sashayed in front of him.

I still didn't understand why the estate plan was so expensive. "It was a complicated estate," said Jerry, "but, I must confess, I was trying to control everything from the grave. I saw the business as being more than it was and had contingencies that just weren't necessary. The trusts had trusts. I was a legend in my own mind.

"I recovered from trying to be such a control freak," said Jerry. "My priorities are finally evolving. My only true wish was to spend winters in Florida. My wife Bobbi's health challenges meant frequent visits to the ER, and I didn't want her to go through another Chicago winter. We didn't know anything about cities in Florida. Before I moved down there, I thought it was a state for alligators, pythons and old people. I was 73 at the time."

After renting for two years, they decided on Weston because it was a new city and had bike lanes. There they found a new estate lawyer in a one-story building. "Your will is a masterpiece," he said, "but the value of your company's assets isn't what they were when this plan was written."

For the eight-page revised will Jerry paid $2,000. "Bobbi had been furious about the price of the previous will. With this version I was finally out of the doghouse."

If I had a hyperactive child, I would find Jerry Horwitz a great comfort. At 83, he is still a jitterbug: swimming, hiking, biking, going to Rotary meetings, running his wealth management business and generally driving his much-beloved wife Bobbi nuts.

This all came to a halt last summer when he had a drug reaction to his blood pressure medication.

He was home alone when his tongue started to swell. Taking an antihistamine didn't reduce the swelling so he called Bobbi to meet him at the Cleveland Clinic (in Florida). "I attribute my survival to finding a good parking space at the hospital," he said. "Calling an ambulance never crossed my male mind."

When Bobbi arrived, Jerry was unconscious. "If you die," she whispered in his ear, "I'm never speaking to you again." Ten doctors crowded the room as she signed the papers to put him in a medically-induced coma.

"I was as nuts in a coma as I am out," said Jerry. "I did my very best to pull the tube out of my throat. I am usually more successful in my endeavors. They had to tie me down to extubate me and bring me out of the coma. I'm sure the nurses thought that I was worse to care for than Hannibal Lector. When I awoke four days later, I asked, 'Where am I?' I knew I wasn't really sick. I was just choking to death. While I was in the hospital fourteen restaurants called because I hadn't been there to eat and they feared bankruptcy."

Jerry's talk grows serious. "Before the coma, I lived like an adolescent," he said. "I would take part in risky sports like scuba diving and participate in all kinds of shenanigans. When I woke up, I was an adult. I have to accept my age. I can't do ten things in a day anymore. Before the coma I thought I was bullet-proof. This was the first time in my life I felt vulnerable."

I knew Jerry was going to be all right when I called him post-hospitalization.

"While I was in a coma," he said, "a baby was born at the hospital that was both male and female."

"How could that be?" I asked.

"It had a brain and a penis."

Welcome back, Jerry.

Had Jerry been born in New York 83 years ago instead of Chicago, he could have taken a different career path as a Borscht Belt comedian. Among his quips:

About his seven years in the Navy: "I had pyorrhea, diarrhea, gonorrhea all in Korea … Well, actually not gonorrhea, but it rhymes."

"I have silver in my hair, gold in my teeth and lead in my bottom."

His repartee with his wife sounds like a Burns and Allen routine. (If you are too young to remember them, Google their names or ask Alexa. She'll know.)

The couple met on a blind date. Jerry was immediately attracted to her sassiness. They were married six months later. "Bobbi suffered from PMS: putting up with men's shit. She makes me laugh all the time."

Which is probably one of the reasons the couple has been married since 1964. "When we get what we ordered, a lot of people aren't happy with the dish," said Jerry. "My dishy wife is perfect. I owe her a lot and appreciate her more than ever." Equally admiring, Bobbie calls her husband "a jewel in the rough."

The couple discusses their philanthropic choices, but they never disagree on them. "When we first married, we argued about money. We didn't have any, so I went into this male state of control. Finally, I came to my senses and turned everything over to her."

After years as a biochemist, Jerry became a financial advisor. "The best part of the work has been helping friends give away millions of dollars they've earned. I got where I was in life because of the generosity of others. I like sharing this concept with friends and clients." He also shares with them his deepest, darkest philanthropy secret. "I like donor-advised funds because I can hide my gifts from Bobbi." (A **donor-advised fund** is a charitable giving vehicle created to manage charitable donations on behalf of organizations, families, or individuals. The main purpose for many is to get the tax deduction at a specific time, rather than to deceive one's spouse!)

Bobbi likes to give to organizations that have had a direct influence on her life, particularly causes that affect her children and grandchildren. When Jerry thinks about philanthropy, he thinks about his grandchildren too, but in a different way.

Ten years ago, he created a group he called Cousins in Philanthropy. The group comprised his eight grandchildren, who could join when they became 10 years old. Jerry's goal: to breathe new life into his grandchildren through philanthropy. He asked them, "Do you want to do this, or has your grandpa just had a brain fart?" They said that they wanted to get involved, but they were busy. He wanted them involved, so for his 80th birthday, he gave each of them $80 to donate to the charity of their choice. At the birthday party, all the grandchildren described their choices and why they made them. The guests became teary-eyed. Jerry kvelled (which is Yiddish for became overwhelmed). "I was so proud and surprised by the elegance and maturity of these young people—all mine!"

"Before this, Grandpa was just a funny guy," said one of the grandkids. "Now we see a serious side we'd never seen before."

At 81, Bobbi doesn't need a lot of hoopla. She enjoys going out with her family for a Chicago hotdog. But Jerry still likes elaborate events, like his 80th party, where his voice was the loudest. "Jerry sings in the Temple choir," said Bobbi. "He makes a big donation, so they have to let him sing, but they put him in the back row. His voice is tolerable." Jerry disagrees: "Move over, Caruso!"

They look at each other and laugh.

Lessons learned

For nonprofit leaders: Many couples have very different approaches to philanthropy. One spouse might want to see your financial statements, while the other has already made up his or her mind based on services rendered.

Ask the question: In addition to yourself, is there anyone you would like to include in your philanthropic decision-making? Some folks want their children and/or grandchildren involved, some want a professional advisor, and some want a solo decision.

One of my clients had a board member approach a friend for a seven-figure gift during a golf game. When the potential donor returned home and told his very new and very young wife about the request, she hit the roof. Furious that she was not included in the conversation, she ordered her husband to tell his golf buddy that they weren't giving a dime. Her husband reluctantly obeyed. The director of advancement asked that I meet with the new wife. I called her, and we hit it off immediately. "I know what it's like to be a trophy wife," I said to her. "The difference between us is that you won first prize." When she agreed to meet, I flew out the next day. I asked her, "How to you want to be seen in the community?"

"I want to be respected," she said. "That approach was disrespectful."

"Do you want to be known as the woman who prevented a hospital wing to be built or one who takes a leadership role?"

After a three-hour conversation, the woman told her husband to double the gift and to tell everyone she had thought the initial request wasn't enough.

Steward not only the current generation of donors but work with the next generations as well. Help the new generation of donors find opportunities to give time and money.

For donors: You and those in your life don't have to agree on what you value but keeping the lines of communication open is important. One family I worked with had a major dispute about giving to "a kill animal shelter." The kids wanted the donations to go to a "no-kill shelter." The parents thought of themselves as pragmatic; the children viewed them as heartless. The family made several field trips before they reached a decision. They also wound up with two new dogs.

Children benefit more from giving time than money. They might not remember how much they gave, but they will remember talking to a homeless man about his time in the army, or how it felt to paint a wall, knowing that a child would enjoy the bright yellow walls. Working with their hands makes a greater impact than giving money, which is an adult concept.

Bringing another generation into the giving process is a fascinating exercise. A client of mine was the oldest of a family of nine. She grew up in a former coal mining town where jobs were few and far between and depression and alcoholism were rampant. She managed to get out of town, get an education and became enormously wealthy. She helped her siblings get through college. The one sorrow in her life was that she and her husband could not have children. We were having dinner one night and she said that she would like to share her values with her nieces and nephews, rather than being a Disneyland Auntie and just buy them presents. Taking a page from Jerry's playbook, I suggested that she get everyone together, give them a lump sum to give away, and present it to the "family elders" for final approval. She followed up immediately. She brought the entire clan together on the 4th of July. The first year she put $10,000 on the table, named the oldest the chair, and put the fifteen kids in a room with a computer. Five hours later, the cousins brought everyone back together. They outlined what they wanted to do, why and even suggested a leadership plan to rotate the chairmanship, with the next oldest chairing the following year until the "baby" who was seven would ultimately chair the proceedings and then back to the oldest. Later, she learned that there had been some serious arguing, yelling, but no fisticuffs, which was a relief. They have been doing this for at least ten years. The entire meeting is endowed in her will with an eight-figure gift. She gave the group the governance responsibility of deciding if spouses and the next generation were invited to the meeting. (They were all invited to the hotel where the meeting took place, on her nickel.) The 4th of July became everyone's favorite holiday.

Celebrate special occasions like weddings, anniversaries and birthdays by including a philanthropic element. When dealing with children, don't push them into giving. Their first experiences with philanthropy should not evoke a sense of loss or intimidation. It is a mistake to ask children to give up their toys before they are ready or to ask for donations in lieu of birthday presents. Giving should feel joyous rather than painful. You have probably had both experiences!

Lindsay Matush at a refugee camp in Burundi, Africa.

— 8 —

The Evolution of a Philanthropist
Lindsay Matush

It was a total setup, and everyone knew it. But it worked every time.

Wealth advisor Jim Matush told his two-year-old daughter Lindsay to ask each of his friends on meeting them, "May I please have a penny?" At the same time Jim counseled each friend to answer Lindsay's question with another one, "What are you going to do with the penny?"

Lindsay was well rehearsed in her answer: "I will invest it in a diversified portfolio."

From early childhood, Lindsay was taught two things: the value of a dollar and the importance of generosity. Wealth was to be shared. Although her parents were affluent, they were prudent when it came to giving their children money. Along with her younger brother Jamie, Lindsay was given three piggy banks with three instructions: the first 10% goes to charity; the next 25%, to savings; and the rest, you get to spend. Someday, their parents added, you will learn that the 65% is what you live on.

The Matushes promised to match their children's savings dollar for dollar. The result was that the kids always found ways to make money. When Lindsay was seven, she and her brother earned a penny for each pesky pinecone that coated the never-ending supply on the lawn of their estate. Every fall, said Lindsay, "We'd literally pick up hundreds and hundreds."

From the age of 10, she babysat. On the weekends, she traipsed to the office with her dad, so that while her father's colleagues worked, she babysat their kids.

Even on family vacations in Colorado, Lindsay and her younger brother earned money bussing tables and bagging groceries.

"I knew from a young age that I was capable of earning money," said Lindsay. "I was always squirreling away my loot."

By the time she was 16, she'd saved $1,000 to buy her first car at an auction. "The car fell apart piece-by-piece, "she said, "but I learned two valuable lessons. First, many of the kids I worked with needed their earnings to put food on the family table, not to stash in a bank account or to buy luxury items. Second, when you buy cheap, sometimes you get what you pay for."

When Lindsay was 21 and working for a nonprofit, she wanted to buy a house in Joplin, Missouri, that cost $54,000. "One of my friends was buying a house, and I liked the idea of home ownership. But working at a nonprofit, I wasn't making hedge fund-type money, so I asked my dad for money as a loan to avoid private mortgage insurance. On one hand, asking my parents for money felt shameful. On the other hand, it seemed like a small thing for them that would give me a big leg up. It would have meant a lot if they'd said yes, and I was disappointed they wouldn't even consider it. I was disappointed but not surprised. It had a long-term effect on me in that I found it easy to ask for help for others, but not myself. Although growing up a Matush with such an emphasis on "earn your way," I knew before the suggestion left my lips what the answer would be."

"The upside was that, for the rest of my life, I had the alternate gift of being able to tell everyone that by the age of 21 I'd bought my first house with my own money. That pride and independence may have been more valuable than a $15,000 down payment."

While working for a nonprofit in Joplin, Lindsay severed a tendon in her finger. She found herself with huge medical bills, little money, and no health insurance. Again, she asked her parents for help. And again, they said, "See what you can do on your own."

Lindsay explained her plight to the surgeon, who cut his bill in half. She zeroed out her bank account. Then she approached the financial aid people at the hospital, who suggested applying for Medicaid. When she was declined, she took her application paperwork to the hospital, which agreed to an installment plan. "My parents never paid a penny," she said. And once again, she learned a valuable lesson from their saying no: "I have not been without insurance a single day since."

"Since I grew up in an affluent family, people sometimes make assumptions, such as 'Daddy bought your life' or 'your parents made it easy.' No question, my parents gave me advantages. Over the years I've seen many friends struggle with college debts, which is something I never had. One of the greatest gifts I ever received was an education paid for by college funds set up by my parents and great-grandparents.

"But the knowledge that I *earned* the material things I have has always contributed to my self-confidence and dignity."

If half of Lindsay's wealth story was learning to value money and earning it herself, the other half was learning to be generous. Her parents included Lindsay and Jamie in their giving conversations and took them along to fundraisers, where they were often the only kids in the room.

As a family, the Matushes served food at a homeless shelter on a regular basis and every Christmas adopted a family for whom they provided gifts. Lindsay played and prayed with the children. Lindsay also taught at an afternoon program for homeless children, which she found gratifying, but in a different way than earning money for her material needs. It was from the heart.

When Lindsay and her brother turned 13, their parents gave each of them $1,000 to give to the charity of their choice.

As a young adult working in Joplin, Lindsay continued the family tradition and served dinner at a homeless shelter every Sunday evening. "I really began to know the residents. I was shy and timid, living my life as a quiet observer. I wouldn't stick up for myself, but I grew up sticking up for the underdog.

Another theme had also been developing in her life. When Lindsay was in seventh grade, her mom became a Christian and the rest of the family followed. "I fell in love with God when I was 13," said Lindsay. "That's how I found myself in the nonprofit world."

That was also how she found herself at 13 on a summer mission trip to build an orphanage in Malawi. The first three weeks she spent in boot camp in Florida with 18 other teenagers from the U.S. and Canada. She signed up to go to Malawi to work, teach and play with children at an orphanage. At the last minute, the assignment was changed, and she was to build an orphanage in a different location.

At training camp in Florida, she was the youngest in the group and weighed 95 pounds, Lindsay had to get up at 6 a.m., run an obstacle course, then perform manual labor all day in 90-degree heat. She was totally unprepared.

On reading Lindsay's letters, her horrified parents thought she had joined a cult. They jumped in the car and drove to Florida to rescue her. Her parents calmed down when they talked to the people in charge who shared that this kind of discipline was needed to build an orphanage. They gave me the option to stay or go, "but I knew I'd always wonder what might have been."

"It was a far cry from the estate I grew up on that was once the home of a beer baron," she said. "I cried every day during training.

But she headed with the others to Malawi for five weeks.

"But once my feet hit the ground in Malawi, I felt happier and more alive than I had in my whole life. I was captivated by the spirit and warmth of the people. Malawi is called the warm heart of Africa. My heart still beats with theirs.

"Living among people who live in extreme poverty changes you for a lifetime. I bathed in a river and washed my clothes in a bucket. The bathroom was a hole in the ground.

There is nothing quite so grounding in what it means to be human than not having a toilet, which most of the world doesn't have. Never again would I take running water for granted. I left my shyness in Malawi."

The transformative mission also gave Lindsay a purpose: "It made me realize my great passion to be of service to others. It was then that I decided to be a doctor and work in Africa."

Life shattered her plans. Three years after she returned from the mission, her beloved brother Jamie died in a rock-climbing accident. "You just don't have a way to process this at 16. My whole world fell apart."

Over the next few years, there were three more deaths in her family. "The worst was that of my grandmother. We were on a family trip to Israel when she died snorkeling in the Red Sea. I thought she was just floating. I went over to help her into the boat. I realized she was dead. I felt frozen in time. Once again, I felt devastated."

To honor their son's life, the Matushes founded a faith-based nonprofit organization, which featured a recreation center connecting teens to both sports activities and adult mentors.

Using the Joplin organization as a model, they set about to replicated the idea in St. Louis. It was called The Bridge. At the time Lindsay was a student at Washington University, so she decided to take a year off to work as an intern for her parent's nonprofit. Lindsay decided that medicine was not for her and decided her mission was to take The Bridge national and switched to marketing. After graduation, she spent five years working 80-hour weeks for The Bridge. Unfortunately, it was not a sustainable model and the St. Louis project never came to be. The Matush family eventually dropped their affiliation with The Bridge in Joplin for philosophical reasons.

Burnout came at 26. Remembering her life-changing experience in Malawi, Lindsay decided to travel to the African nations of Rwanda and Burundi, as well as to Southeast Asia. "Have a good time," her parents said, "but get your will written before you go."

"I was not afraid of death," said Lindsay. "And I had spent a lot of time studying spirituality, so writing my first will in my 20s was a fun way to have friends celebrate my life. I left my house to a friend who worked for a nonprofit. The rest I set up as a fund to be directed by my closest friend. I spelled out the parameters: ministries with a faith-based mission that were close to my heart. I wanted to serve refugees in this life and the next."

While many of her peers spent their leisure time abroad hiking the Alps or strolling the Champs-Elysees in Paris, Lindsay headed to the refugee camps in East Africa.

There she got to know a stateless tribe of Congolese refugees, who had been driven from their lands. "They were so gaunt," she said, "and yet they were joyful and generous. One woman gave me one of her few dresses. As these people described the massacre at Gatumba, a U.N.-sanctioned camp where they had lived, they cried, and I cried with them. When I asked what I could do to help, one said, 'Tell our story, and tomorrow we will feel more whole because you have shared our pain.'

"Once again, I was faced with no plumbing, but their hospitality was beyond belief. Through them, I learned the beauty of sharing."

Today, the Tribe is in her will. One member of the tribe, Justin, made his way to the U.S. and lives in St. Louis, has become a close friend. "He calls me sister. I feel I have a brother again."

"The Tribe in general and particularly my friend Justin, have helped me reframe my thoughts on asking. Until I met them, I felt uncomfortable asking anyone for money, which included charitable gifts for the causes I support. But these people just call and ask unashamedly when they or a loved one has a need, knowing that they will be there for the other person if their largess is required later. I know there are plenty of scams, but when you are known, it is entirely transparent. These people hold money much more open-handedly. It has made me rethink how I give. And it has made me more generous."

To assist others in structuring their generosity, five years ago Lindsay founded Vario Philanthropy, named after an instrument used by hang-glider pilots to measure change. "I was raised as an adventure hound and went hang-gliding with dad from the time I was seven. I know it is inherently dangerous, but I love the adrenaline rush, and I feel at peace in nature."

Helping others articulate and execute their philanthropic intentions reminded Lindsay that her own will needs an update—a classic case of the shoemaker's child going barefoot. "When I sit down to rewrite my estate plan, which always seems to be on the back burner, I will restructure it differently using the tools I've used working with other families." Her beneficiaries are "five organizations that are close to my heart and people I care deeply about."

Today, at 34, "My life has not turned out anything like I'd imagined," she said. "I thought I'd be a physician living in Africa, with a husband and kids. I'd still love to be married and have children, but if the right guy doesn't come along, life as a single woman will continue to be full.

"I love my life, my faith and my work. I stumbled on the perfect business: helping others with their philanthropy. There is so much more to learn and so much exciting work ahead."

Lessons learned

Note: The response by my team of friends and proofreaders has been extreme. One upper-middle class attorney said, "I wish I had been more like Lindsay's parents. If my

45-year-old son doesn't want money, I don't hear from him. He is no more independent than when he was three and I can see the part I played in it."

A friend who is a surgeon exploded. "If this woman was from a family with money and wouldn't help her with her medical bills, I think they should be shot. I have fourteen years of post-high school training. I have undergraduate bills as well as medical school loans. I am a single mother with two teenagers who are starting to look at college. I have patients who are truly indigent. I care for them for free. The surgeon should not have had to reduce his fee because someone had tight-fisted parents." The ranting went on, and most of her language is not for public consumption.

And finally, a friend who works in retail said, "When my aunt died and left me money, the first thing I thought of was that I could help my son and daughter-in-law buy a house. My grandson would have a yard and not concrete to play on. What is money for if not to share with loved ones?" An interesting aspect of this story is that her daughter-in-law came up with the idea of buying a duplex so that they could live close to one another. Her son said, "We want our kids to learn German from you and how to bake your addictive Christmas cookies and we want to be there for you if you need anything when you are a grouchy old lady."

For nonprofit leaders: Lindsay is a young woman. One day, she will also be an heiress. Don't assume that young people haven't had poignant, life-changing experiences or that they don't have real wisdom. Listen and learn. Many are awed by their IT skills. There is a lot more to them.

You have to find a way to bring your potential donors to your mission. It might be through a film. If your mission focuses on the developmentally disabled, one of my favorite movies to share is *Riding The Bus With My Sister*. Although it is an old film, *The Burning Bed* portrays a great deal of wisdom about spousal abuse. Just ask your favorite film buff. There are movies about everything from race relations, to the inhumanity of man, to the rigors of producing an opera. Be careful what you choose. *Schindler's List* is not the film to proceed an evening of dinner and dancing. You need to schedule time to discuss and share what you saw.

Another great way to share the importance of your work is a mission trip. It can be a one-day visit to the local Boys and Girls Club or two weeks in the Holy Land.

For donors: Take a risk. Go into areas that might scare you.

A businessman in his late 30s told me that he didn't want to live "a gated life," so I recruited him for the board of a nonprofit that cared for people with HIV. I arranged for him to meet with the nonprofit's executive director, as well as the care team at a medical center in the Bronx. We also had lunch with five people—three women and two men—with HIV. All had been prostitutes. They chatted and laughed as they told him their horrific life stories. He didn't know what to think. I asked him if he wanted to take some time to decide about joining the board. He said yes, and we agreed that I would call him in a week.

By the time he got back to his office on Wall Street, he looked seriously shaken. I imagine the soldiers who discovered the concentration camps post-World War II had the same haunted look. His coworkers urged him to find a less "distasteful charity," perhaps something like a children's museum. When he talked to his wife that night, he told her how scared he had been in the Bronx.

"Did you learn anything?" she asked.

"Yes. To be a prostitute, it turns out that you don't have to be attractive—you can be missing teeth. And you don't even have to be a woman."

The couple talked into the night about their life of privilege and what they took for granted. The next morning, over breakfast, they continued the conversation.

"Does this work really scare you?" his wife asked.

"Yes."

"Then man up and do it," she said.

Within a month, he was working a night shift from midnight to 5 a.m., during which he handed out sandwiches and condoms to sex workers. He later told me, "I learned more in that first night about who I was and what I had in common with humanity, than I did in all my years at prep school, Dartmouth and Wharton. Thank you."

When to open one's wallet and when to keep it shut is a conundrum all parents deal with at some time. These are not easy decisions, especially when parents disagree. Wisdom is hard won in this familial battle whether you have great wealth or very little money.

The Jenkins Family

– 9 –

Sudden Wealth and Charitable Giving
Phil and Sharon Jenkins

Phil Jenkins' two younger daughters couldn't decide what to give their dad for Christmas. Their quandary was understandable. Their older sister, Amie, had given him a kidney. What greater gift can you give than a piece of yourself, literally and figuratively?

Post-transplant, Phil's life has changed. He now sets his alarm for 7:30 a.m. to take his "don't die" pills. He never complains. Whining is not an acceptable form of speech in the Jenkins family. His wife, Sharon, says that no one pays attention anyway. They are a warm but stoic clan.

Phil hadn't realized that he was in trouble. The only sign that his kidneys weren't functioning came from a routine lab test, which he flunked with a capital F. His doctors monitored him and eventually started dialysis. Because he was over 70, Phil knew he would be last on the transplant list. His brother volunteered to be a donor but was not a good match. Phil was on dialysis for 15 months when his oldest daughter surprised him by saying, "What if I were the donor?"

Before the transplant, Phil was so fatigued that he couldn't take his 11 grandchildren to the family farm ten miles outside of town. (I don't know a lot of healthy people over 70 who could corral 11 kids, but that is another matter.)

The 135-year-old farmhouse meant a lot to Phil. His grandmother was born there, and the family managed to hold onto the 100-acre property through the Depression. Phil cherished its history and lifestyle—the cattle, the hay and the deer hunting. Until his kidney problems he raised Longhorn cows. The farmhouse is habitable, but all cooking is done on a wood stove. There is no electricity on the farm, which means no air conditioning. We are talking East Texas, not known for its pleasant summers. And no running water, therefore, no showers or commodes. Phil wanted to imprint this world gone by on his grandchildren and bought out his siblings, so he could do just that.

Every year Phil invites his grandkids for boys-only or girls-only weekends. He has taught them to fish and tried to teach them how to squirrel hunt, but that was a joke since the children had to be quiet for at least five minutes. Instead, he concentrated on teaching them to target shoot. The farm was not only a safe place for squirrels but a magical place for the children.

And a magical place for Phil. Thanks to his renewed energy after the transplant, he can now go to the farm again with the kids. Phil can barely talk about what it means to be able to visit his much-loved farm. Tears and faltering speech tell it all.

"I wonder if I would have donated one of my kidneys," he said. "I'm not sure I would have."

His wife spoke up, "I'm absolutely sure he would have."

The transplant has changed their lives. But it isn't the first dramatic change the couple has experienced. Years earlier, Phil's family sold their company, of which he was the CFO. The Jenkins' oil field service business cleared land for companies that wanted to drill. In the early days, the business cleared areas with mules and moved stumps by hand. By the time Phil joined the team, they were using bulldozers and ditching machines. Over the years, many companies offered to buy the Jenkins' business, but the family was patient, and by waiting until they all agreed the time was right, the sale was a big one. Phil was 59.

The best part of selling? "Disconnecting my alarm clock," said Phil. "It is back on because of my 'do not die pills,' but I control the time, and it isn't O-dark-thirty anymore."

The sudden wealth was, at first, sheer fun—the first time in their lives they felt affluent. After the check was safely in the bank, Sharon says, "We headed straight for the Mercedes dealership. And who should we meet there?

The man who handled the sale of our company. I guess we all had a great day." Phil, not to be outdone, bought an airplane. When he talks about it, there is rapture in his voice, "It was a Piper Dakota ... not too sexy, but would take 4 people with luggage to any small (or large) airport in the Western hemisphere ...

His wife Sharon chimed in, "In addition to a plane and a new car, We were able to take the whole family on some pretty terrific cruises. We enjoyed being able to give more to our church. Our lives really didn't change much other than that. We lived in the same house. I cooked the same meals. Life went on pretty much as usual."

But soon it became a challenge, because neither Phil nor Sharon had come from money. They both grew up in the tiny town of Palestine, Texas, where they met in high school and married soon after. The town had a movie theater and a non-integrated community swimming pool. Sharon had a little experience with big city living because her father worked for the railroad, sometimes out of Houston, and sometimes out of Palestine so they moved from time to time, but ultimately, their town of 12,000 was home.

Phil was the first person in his family to graduate from college and as such he didn't know a whole lot about how it worked. He was enrolled in the business school at the University of Texas at Austin but wasn't getting good grades until he took accounting. He didn't know what a CPA was, but when he got an "A" in the course, he'd found his field. After graduation, he practiced as a CPA. Sharon went to UT-Austin for two years, then quit to work at a bank in Amarillo. It turned out, they both liked to eat!

The couple still lives in Palestine, which today boasts a population of 18,000, a six-screen movie theater, and an integrated swimming pool at the YMCA. "We love our little town," says Sharon, "and we've decided our giving will stay local. We certainly don't think of ourselves as philanthropists. Giving is just what people do."

But how much to give and to whom became an ongoing dilemma. "We want to get credit for a gift," said Phil, "but then we got bombarded for additional requests. It was all very new to us."

Their church, First Methodist, was a top priority. They also gave and recruited others to give to the University of Texas-Tyler in Palestine. In 2017 they won The Visionary Award in honor of their philanthropy to the city.

Giving anything more than $1,000, the Jenkins decided, would be a decision they made as a couple, with one notable exception. When a longtime attorney friend was asked what amount he was donating to First Methodist, he replied, "I'm going to give what Phil gives." Phil, on his own, immediately doubled the couple's donation. With a soft spot for the rascal in Phil, Sharon was fine with this decision.

Sharon's passion was to fund scholarships. "I had to go to work and wasn't able to finish college. I know that many kids in our town are in the same position. I love when I can make someone's educational dream come true."

Phil, too, is interested in bettering children's lives, particularly through kindergarten programs. He found inspiration in the bestseller *A Hillbilly Elegy* by J.D. Vance. The author had nothing growing up but then worked hard and became wealthy and decided to do good with his money.

Phil believes that philanthropy is the enemy of inheritance. He knows that the more he gives away, the less they will have to leave to their children. "We plan to die broke," says Sharon. "Our kids are well on their way and don't need us. They aren't rich, but they have plenty.

They've paid for college for their children but have decided that the eleven tuitions for the grandchildren are the responsibility of their daughters and their husbands. Phil is proud that all three of his girls have stayed married to their first husbands and that all three families live within their means.

Sharon and Phil try hard to be fair with their children, which doesn't always mean equal. The donation of the kidney has never come into the equation. According to Sharon, "If Amie wants to reclaim it, that would be another matter."

After his transplant, Phil built a zip line on the farm. The grandkids liked it so much, he built another one at their home in town. Let's face it, what grandchild complains of too many zip lines?

Today, Phil and Sharon, married 51 years, are still enjoying their sudden wealth, spending it on things that are "not inexpensive, but not crazy." The recent family cruise to Alaska is a typical splurge. "We all had such a great time planning it," said Sharon, "even though I broke both of my knee caps taking a stroll a few months before. I was sheathed in two straight-leg casts, which meant I couldn't get into a car, so I was housebound except when a medical transport vehicle took me to the orthopedic surgeon in the next town. I told myself, 'This too shall pass.'

"Our family is of the action-Jackson school of travel. Everyone wanted to climb glaciers and hike, but with my bum knees I stayed at the buffet on the ship and ate. But I was determined to keep a good disposition and not whine. I enjoyed being away from the house after being trapped for so long. Every night we would meet, the kids having dinner with us old people. The fun was when they told stories of their day.

"That is what being rich is all about. Having dinner with the family and telling stories, whether on an elegant ship cruising Alaska or at our big old dinner table in our little hometown."

Lessons learned

For nonprofit leaders: This is a family with a finely-tuned philanthropic philosophy and family mission. If you are a charity in Palestine, Texas and help local people, you are going to get a check. If you are a big national or international charity, save your breath. Some donors have an eclectic and sometimes erratic choice of nonprofits. The Jenkins know who they are and how they are going to give—end of story.

It is not uncommon for well-grounded people to purchase a few luxuries when faced with sudden wealth but keep the same values. Initial euphoria gives way to responsibilities and questions: How much should we give and to whom? Do we want recognition, and if so, in what form? What is wise and fair when giving to family members?

For donors: It is difficult and time-consuming to develop a clear philosophy of giving when you don't hail from generations of wealth. You want to be recognized, but then you can become a target for donations, so you want to be anonymous, but then you want to set an example, and so it goes until you find the right balance in how you give, whom you give to and what you want in terms of recognition.

If you have children, you must be clear when to open your checkbook and when to keep it closed. This again presents challenges. What is enough? What is too much? The Jenkins have decided that money will be spent on family adventures, whether on their nearby farm or in exotic locations like Alaska. And when you put this kind of love and thought into giving, don't be surprised when a child gives you a kidney and saves your life.

The indomitable Susan Ellis, preparing for her fourth round of chemotherapy.

— 10 —

Leaving More Than Money
Susan J. Ellis

Susan Ellis has been living with cancer for the last seven years. Because she was told at the very start that her prognosis was bleak, she immediately updated her will.

This was nothing new for Susan. She'd been updating her will on a regular basis with each new life circumstance. Susan wrote her first one at 22—a simple will crafted by an estate-planning lawyer. She had just graduated from Temple University in Philadelphia, where she was planning to stay and work. Her parents lived in New Jersey.

Most new college graduates don't think of wills, but Susan's relationship with her parents was exceptionally close. "In case something happened," she said, "I couldn't imagine not sharing my final wishes with my parents. We were a very tight unit."

The only child of Holocaust survivors, Susan understood the fragility of life from an early age. All four of her grandparents, as well as aunts, uncles and cousins, had died in concentration camps. The relatives who escaped their native Austria were dispersed around the world. Susan's parents were spared the fate of others because her father had skills as a tool and die maker. This expertise secured them a special visa to escape to Australia, where they lived for nine years before immigrating to the U.S. to be closer to Susan's mother's brother.

Within six months of settling in Manhattan—when Susan's mother was 38 and her father 47—they were delighted by their news of a late-life baby, especially because Australian doctors had diagnosed her mother as infertile. Susan has been surprising people ever since.

By the time Susan was 30, her father had died. Ten years later, the relatives who'd escaped the camps were all dead, too.

Professionally, Susan wanted a job working with delinquent children. She found a position with the Philadelphia Family Court in a prevention program requiring a community volunteer program. At age 23 with no volunteer management training, the top executive figured she'd be fine for this role! In her five and a half years in this job, she fell in love with the program's volunteers, eventually began to train other leaders of volunteers in other agencies in the city.

In 1977, Susan founded Energize, Inc. to assist organizations of all types—health, human service, cultural arts, schools, business, government agencies—to start or strengthen their volunteer involvement. Knowing how little had been written on the subject, she co-authored *By the People: A History of Americans as Volunteers* (by Susan J. Ellis and Katherine Noyes Campbell, now in its third edition).

"There have always been volunteers," said Susan. "Let's face it, volunteers built Noah's Ark. But there were no professional management guides."

Between the 25 books Energize published and Susan's continuing invitations to provide training to others on the subject, her career continued to widen. Over the next decades, she worked with clients across North America, Latin America, Europe, Asia, and Australia and New Zealand.

When her company took off, she again updated her will, naming the individuals she wanted her executor to approach to take over the company in the event of her death. "My parents certainly didn't want the business and there needed to be a succession plan. I also wanted to make sure that my authors would never lose their copyrights."

When Susan married in 1984, she went back to her attorney for an estate update. Given that her husband had three children by a previous marriage, she wanted to make sure that her mother would be taken care of. Seven years later, when the couple divorced, Susan again headed to her lawyer's office to update her will.

It was about this time—in the mid-1990s—that I met Susan. We were both on the faculty of the Learning Institute for Nonprofit Organizations. Every year for five years, we filmed a series of lectures for PBS. I'll never forget the first faculty meeting. Susan and I come from similar stock and both look like little dumplings, though Susan has black hair and I am a bottle-redhead. Another significant difference between us: Although we were both 48 at the time, she was at the top of her field and internationally known; I had started my company just three years earlier, which made me a novice, intimidated by the rest of the faculty.

Susan was a major alpha female and brilliant. I liked her immediately. She kept asking the director a barrage of relevant questions: Who is going to be listening to these broadcasts? Professionals? Newcomers? What assumptions should we make regarding their skill level? Will this be aired in other countries where the content would need to be broader to include cultural differences? Would this be shown with subtitles? If so, would we be able to work with the translators? The director didn't know a single answer and was clearly under-medicated to do battle with Susan. The entire faculty recognized that this guy was out of his league. Perry Mason was an amateur when it came to interrogating this unprepared witness. As the director's sweat stains dripped almost to his waist, it dawned on me that I had not thought of one of Susan's audience-focused questions. For the first time in three years, I really understood what it meant to understand one's audience. A gigantic lightbulb shone over my head.

What I came to most appreciate about Susan was that, during down time, she generously coached me and continues to do so to this day. There was no question that I couldn't ask her, and I usually had a myriad of consulting, publishing and speaking questions.

When I was having trouble getting paid for international speaking gigs and aware that Susan was speaking all over the world, I asked how she got the international clients to pay. "I don't always get paid," she said. "I love to travel, but, as a single woman, I would have had to pay a supplementary charge for a single room, sit at the back of a bus and hope that some kind couple invited me to join them for dinner. Obviously, this setup was not appealing. Since this was the International Year of the Volunteer, I let it be known that for one year I would speak anywhere if I didn't have to open my wallet."

In the following years, negotiating these overseas trips, Susan would mention that if a client had someone who would put her up for a few days, she would love to see the country and would lower her fee based on this travel opportunity. "My clients were thrilled to have some extra consulting time, and I loved seeing the country through their eyes. The result was that for talking about one of my favorite subjects—helping organizations make the most of their resources—I was picked up at airports around the world, feted and housed in people's homes, and given so many presents that I often had to buy another suitcase to bring them all home."

I had made friends with a genius, a bold one at that. And I've continued to learn from her, most recently about setting short-term goals as we age.

When Susan's mother died of Alzheimer's in 2004 and Susan no longer needed to set aside funds for her care, she once again headed to the office of her estate lawyer, who by now had been with her 40 years (and still is).

Much as she wanted to keep her life's work alive, Susan had no heirs and didn't think anyone else would want to run her 30-year-old company. So, she chose a group of friends and colleagues who agreed to be on a transition committee if her health failed. Their charge was to make sure that Susan's efforts to support volunteer management—her legacy—continued, in whatever form they saw fit.

When diagnosed with cancer in 2011, Susan changed her will again, asking her transition committee to ensure the future for her library on volunteerism, one of the largest in the world. The library consists of: Susan's writings on the subject, which comprise 17 books, chapters in other books, journal and newspaper articles; other people's work on volunteerism in various languages; articles and books from other authors that Energize has published; the libraries and archives of two of her late mentors; and the company's comprehensive website Energizeinc.com, which contains thousands of pages on volunteerism. As both a teaching and archival organization, Energize has captured the centuries-spanning trajectory of thought leaders in the field.

Because Susan has a large selected "family" but no living relatives, she is working on a plan to leave her life's work to the volunteer sector. The easy choice would have been to sell the company and donate the money to a volunteer organization. As an alpha female, an entrepreneur and a community builder, however—not to mention a teeny tiny bit of a control freak about how few of the large organizations deploy their volunteers well—she is seeking an alternative path.

In her most recent will, Susan and her various consulting staff decided that, while the publishing and training work of Energize could continue as a business, the company's large resource archive needed to continue as a nonprofit to serve the volunteer sector. In December 2018, she bequeathed money to ensure that a transition committee explores what to do with her life work, and what form Energize should take in the future, and how to raise money for such services.

The cancer was "supposed" to end Susan's life in five years, but she was noncompliant. At the first symptom in 2011, she didn't futz around Googling symptoms or ignoring them. She went immediately to a doctor. A hysterectomy and a round of chemo and radiation brought two years of remission, but the cancer returned in her lymph nodes. A determined warrior who still had things to do, she marched back to the chemo chair. Last year she was accepted into a drug trial for her kind of cancer, and while the treatment helped her cancer it also caused a brain tumor.

Susan wanted to share how she was doing with her multitude of friends, colleagues, and employees around the world, so she created "Magical Medical Monday," a weekly e-mail blog on her journey through the foibles of our health system. Her column features the views of both an oncologist and her primary doctor, whom Susan calls Saint Lisa. The blog reveals poignant, frustrating and devastating moments and is Oscar Wilde-witty. One of my favorite examples: "If you are one of my male friends and tend to be squeamish, you might want to skip this section because it discusses my lady parts." Those on Susan's mailing list often had something to say and grew to know one another. Said Susan, "One wisenheimer friend wrote, 'The next time I hear you saw a doctor, I want to hear that he bought you dinner and that you were both undressed later.'"

Instead of meeting a neurosurgeon for dinner, Susan met several in the operating room to remove a cancerous brain tumor. The surgery left Susan disoriented and weak, and, in December 2017, she went on hospice. Her executor emailed her friends that it was just a matter of time before an inoperative blood clot in her leg would break off, go to her heart and kill her. Across the world, friends and colleagues felt the blow. I felt that the world would soon lose a force of nature. But Susan is nothing if not full of surprises. After a few months of not dying, she was released from hospice care. Susan is one tough little spud. The question is whether her cancer is more tenacious than she is.

Housebound for almost a year since the latest operation, Susan looks forward to engaging in real life again. "As I continue this mysterious medical journey, I want to feel that I am still contributing to things that matter." If nothing else, she has had more time to plan for the future of Energize, Inc. than she had anticipated.

In reflecting on her life, Susan said she would have loved to have children and a second marriage. But if she had, "I wouldn't have had the opportunity to experience so many people from different cultures. I feel my life has had real meaning. If I had children, I wouldn't have been able to do as much to enhance a field I love. I feel good about my legacy. When I can drive again, I'll feel even better!"

Lessons learned

For nonprofit leaders: Many donors own intellectual property, which can often be a far greater gift than a check with lots of zeros. Probably the most famous example of this type of gift was in 1929 when author J. M. Barrie left the rights to *Peter Pan* to Great Ormond Street Hospital in London. His legacy has provided a significant source of income to the hospital ever since. The rights were supposed to last only 50 years, but Prime Minister Lord Callaghan successfully proposed an amendment to the copyright law granting Great Ormond Street Hospital the right to royalties for all things *Peter Pan*, from peanut butter to films to e-books.

You need a policy about what kind of gifts you are willing to receive. You could find yourself with a piece of land that is a toxic waste site, or an old farmhouse that is an *Antiques Roadshow* dream. Sometimes you have to take the time to really explore unusual gifts such as intellectual property and unique properties. Who would have guessed that a book written decades ago would support sick children when we eat peanut butter?

For donors: We have more to leave behind than a pot of money and the proverbial garage full of junk. We have copyrights. We have patents. We have collections. Some are financially valuable, others offer only sentimental value. Look at your life holistically. If you have children, friends or relatives, find out who wants what. A dear friend of mine was dying and wanted to return the suit I had given her to get married in. I wanted her opera tickets, which she graciously passed on since no one in her family wanted them. These tickets—third-row seats for four—are priceless to our family. Every time we go, I think of her.

Discuss who would want to have a specific item. One pair of mega-millionaires wanted to leave a collection of rare French porcelain to their grown children. But none of the kids wanted to pay for the hefty insurance, plus, one lived in Manhattan and didn't have the space, so the parents bequeathed the collection to an art museum. The couple received a tax deduction as well as the joy of seeing their collection displayed in a room they funded during their lifetime and endowed in their estate plan.

Don't make assumptions. In my case, I no longer fit into the suit I gave my friend, and the art collector's children didn't want their collection. Look for creative ways to share the things that you or your donors have collected and valued. Susan's committee will shepherd the body of work she created for generations to come.

Simone Joyeaux and Tom Ahern on the moors of Southern England.

The Poet and the Planner Give It All Away
Tom Ahern and Simone Joyeaux

I've known families that have their own mission statement, frequently crafted by one family member, usually male, usually old. One such man, a former client, wrote 150 pages on his family's values, vision for the future, and plans for their money. He didn't consult a single family member, and the statement did not allow for changes in the family's circumstances.

Married couple Simone Joyeaux and Tom Ahern, by contrast, have a war cry. Jointly created, it comprises one sentence: "We believe that people eat, sleep, dream and make love in languages other than English, in colors other than ours, and in pairings other than opposite sex," said Simone. "This conviction is what we fight for in our lives, in our work, and in our giving. Our war cry will be our legacy."

Both Tom and Simone are world-renowned speakers, authors and consultants. Tom focuses on donor communications and Simone specializes in fund development, fundraising, board development and strategic planning. Many of us in the field see them as our gurus. I always recommend their books to clients. I am sure that nonprofit groupies offer to carry their luggage when they work in the UK, Norway and other countries. I have never missed a chance to hear them speak. Just when I think I know almost everything, they teach me something new.

The first time I heard Simone speak, many years ago, at an Association for Fundraising Professionals event in New Jersey, she said that, when she and her husband died, all their money was going to charity. I knew I wanted to hear more.

When the couple met, she said, they were both divorced and in their late thirties, so they didn't plan on having children. If it happened, it happened; and if didn't, that was okay. As it turned out, it didn't happen. When Simone asked Tom if he regretted not having children, he said, "No, because we can always have children in our lives, even if we have to rent them."

The couple had lots of relatives with children, so there were plenty of kids to enjoy and "rent" for the afternoon.

After a few such outings, "we were good with being child-less," said Simone.

Simone was working as the chief development officer for a repertory theater and Tom was working in public relations for the State Arts Council in Rhode Island. When she applied for a grant from the Arts Council, she won both the grant and Tom. (They claim there was no collusion!)

Simone and Tom were more pragmatic than romantic, and this wasn't their first rodeo. Tom set the wedding date on his birthday, so he'd always remember it. Simone combed the yellow pages to find a judge, who married them in police court. When the judge said they needed witnesses, they asked six friends to attend. After the ceremony, everyone went back to work. The same efficient, thoughtful planning goes into their philanthropy.

Tom's journey to the world of nonprofits was circu-itous. He started out wanting to be a poet and majored in creative writing at Brown. He found a passion in writing and published short stories and poetry for small presses. The weekend the couple got married, the *New York Times* reviewed his first short story collection. Like his wedding day, Tom envisioned this 100-word positive review as the beginning of something wonderful. What Tom didn't know was that this NYT mention would be the high point of his literary career.

The problem with the literary life was that Tom wanted to live indoors and he wanted to eat, so he worked as an independent contractor, doing such work as writing employee policies. From there he segued to a large corporation, where he wrote proposals for contracts worth $50-100 million.

"That experience changed my view of money," he said. "I got to see what it looked like when the sky was the limit and all that mattered was winning. I had a million-dollar budget and could hire superb staffers, but the pressure was excruciating, and the environment was toxic. I lasted five years.

"But I got the training of a lifetime. After that tech marketing stint, I was never afraid of big projects. I worked for the best, and they insisted that we be the best. The deadlines were unbreakable. You snooze, you lose. With my team, I might write a 500-page proposal that was couriered by private jet to the capital of some exotic country. It was serious, aggressive stuff: All of this after being a poet!

"I needed to find a middle ground between being an impoverished writer and a corporate executive who was part potentate and part drone."

That middle ground turned out to be advertising, where Tom partnered with a friend before going solo. His creativity landed international awards.

As Simone introduced Tom to her nonprofit clients and they began to hire him, he learned about the world of fundraising. "After shilling luxury yachts and roof membranes, nonprofits were a shock. In sales, you either you sell it, or you don't." Tom's firm was hired to do employee communications, 401Ks, and disability insurance. "When I found out that only 1% of the people who had disability insurance cashed in, I felt like I a co-conspirator. I had been living in an ethics-light world."

When Tom entered the nonprofit arena, he expected a lion and found a lamb. And not a frolicking lamb, but a little lost lamb. This was a far cry from the heady days of hiring whomever he needed and spending whatever it took to get the multi-million-dollar contracts.

The transition was rocky. "What shocked me was that in sales, you think about the customer all the time," said Tom. "The nonprofit world didn't have customers. Or, at least, that's what I thought. It took me years to understand that there *was* a customer for fundraising: the donor."

He found the problem was that "there were all these supposed 'best practices.' Executives and board members would just see other people doing something to raise funds, and they'd steal the ideas without realizing the ideas were based on faulty assumptions." He cited as an example the letter from the executive director featured on the front page of every nonprofit newsletter. After reading more than 60 of them, he realized that this prime newsletter real estate was being wasted, because readers assumed it was PR hype and ignored it.

Tom was a trained direct mail writer. But when he brought up direct mail, a board member said that'd been tried and didn't work. "I wanted to say, 'You sent out a lousy letter to a poor list and you don't know anything.' Being a donor doesn't make you an expert on fundraising any more than having an operation makes you a surgeon. It is easy to get it wrong."

Tom needed to integrate what he learned in the corporate marketing world into the nonprofit world. His marketing mentors taught him: "Keep it simple. Write at a grade-school level. Avoid insider language."

Making difficult concepts easily understandable takes work. But it was work the former poet knew how to do. He became the Hemingway of how-to books for nonprofit pros.

Simone said that her own work for nonprofits wouldn't have been as effective without Tom reading— and rewriting—her donor communications. She describes a typical interaction one morning when Tom ambled into her office:

"I don't know how the hell you people ever raised any money," he said.

"Hello, how are you?" said Simone. "And who do you mean by 'you people'?"

"You fundraisers. I read hundreds of donor communications a year and most of it sucks."

"I will tell people that," she said, as she went back to work and Tom ambled back to his office.

Simone's path to the nonprofit industry was both similar and different from Tom's.

Like her husband, she started out as an avid reader and literary lover. She earned a master's in 20th century French and American literature with the idea of becoming a teacher. When she couldn't get a job in her field, she let go of academia and worked as an executive director of a small arts organization. "I was dumb enough and smart enough to apply," she said, "and they were dumb enough and smart enough to hire me. I knew nothing about fundraising, the nonprofit arena or governance. It was all on-the-job training."

From there, Simone moved to Rhode Island to become chief development officer for one of the country's top regional theaters. That's when she met Tom.

"First, I got him into bed and then I got him into the non-profit sector," she said. "Perhaps not an evil plot but definitely serendipity."

When Tom started his own business, Simone got him his first nonprofit client and his first speaking engagement. They co-wrote *Keep your Donors: A guide to better communications and stronger relationships.* "The good news is that we didn't get a divorce over it," said Simone. "We discovered that we have very different work and writing styles.

Which seems surprising given that their natures are similar—both are introverts—and ironic, given their quiet natures, both are performers. They board airplanes every couple of weeks to speak around the world on topics in their shared field. They both carry paper and pen when hiking together in France.

But when it comes to giving, each has their favorite charities to which they give separately. They also have charities to which they give together. These joint causes are the ones reflected in their planned giving.

The community foundation gets about 70% of their estate. "But we have to die first," Simone quips. Designated funds also go to Planned Parenthood of Southern New England, where Simone was the local board chair; The Association of Fundraising Professionals, a community repertory company; Brown University, Tom's alma mater; and a scholarship Simone established.

In her father's name, the scholarship enables a student to enjoy an immersive experience in a French-speaking country. Simone's French-born father, who had emigrated to the U.S. as an adult after World War II, became a professor of French literature at Michigan State, an expert in 20th century existentialists, and a prolific author. "My father taught us that people lived their lives in different manners, that 'different' was beautiful and not something to be feared. He was quoted in a newspaper article saying, 'We have to get out of our linguistic and cultural ghetto.' Honoring my father's beliefs and values became the basis for our war cry. It makes me proud to help young people understand his teachings, which have become my beliefs."

Tom gives to Nyaka, a school for HIV orphans in Uganda. He was impressed, he said, with both the school's founder, whom he met, and the school's donor communications, which continually affirm Tom's value. Vetted by CNN, Nyaka has produced a number of videos from the field showing that every time Nyaka had a problem the school created a solution. By continually filling gaps and moving forward, today Nyaka boasts an elementary school, a high school, a trade school and a hospital.

"I enjoy monthly giving," said Tom, "because it's an ongoing reminder of the charities I support."

Tom also gives to Spectrum Youth and Family Services in Burlington, Vermont, for homeless youth, a group he met at a training session. "I fell in love with their direct mail—the group was gifted in communications and fundraising—so I made a first gift and have continued ever since. I like their way of warmly thanking donors. Their thank-yous don't feel like a tax letter for the IRS."

The couple gives at least 10% of their income to charities. "Philanthropy is our life's work," said Simone. "I believe that I was put on this earth to do the work of social justice."

Lessons learned

For professional staff: If you want to receive ongoing gifts, or get included in an estate plan, people like Tom and Simone are hard nuts to crack. They expect exemplary communications. They want to feel good about their giving.

Tom and Simone are typical of childless people: more of their money has been pledged to charity. If a donor has children, the rate of planned giving to charity goes down to 10%; if there are grandchildren, more like 5%. With childless folks, it is entirely possible that 100% of their estate will be allocated to charity.

Even if donors have children, the quality of the relationship is significant. Be sensitive to any friction or estrangement between parents and children. In these cases, there can be an opportunity for nonprofits to benefit. For an example, in the early 1970s, my cousin joined a cult. She sold her home and car and gave the proceeds along with her emptied bank account to the cult leader. My cousin's mother—my aunt—had given her the down payment for the house and was not happy with the "re-gifting." Ultimately, the mother and daughter ceased communication. When my widowed aunt died seven years later, she gave her entire estate to charity.

Some wealthy families severely limit the inheritance their children receive. The philosophy of certain billionaires, millionaires and even thousandairs is that they want their children to live meaningful lives, and that means working lives.

These folks may have children, but they are loath to give them more than "enough." Since their fortunes are vast, they still give large portions of their estates to causes they espouse.

For donors: If you are childless, create a philosophy of giving and an estate plan that reflects your values. Many people find this exercise both provocative and productive. The questions to ask yourself: What have I done that I can build on? How would I like the world to change after I'm gone?

Bet and Jack Stapleton with healthy brand-new grandchild.

— 12 —

From Heartbreak to Healing
Jack Stapleton

Jack Stapleton is the kind of guy you want for your wealth management advisor. He is the quintessential jovial Irishman, with a keen eye for numbers. In addition to his financial acumen, Jack is the rare combination of a great listener and a great storyteller. I met him through a pediatric support nonprofit. He served on the board. He understood philanthropy and finances. He gave time and money. He asked smart questions. He also looked like someone who could give a great hug if you were in crisis.

The giveaway is that sometimes his smile didn't go up to his eyes.

Jack Stapleton and his wife Bet have led family discussions about the decision that their estate would reflect their philanthropic beliefs. They have allocated the bulk of the charitable giving in their wills to St. Louis Children's Hospital. No development director for another charity, no matter how ambitious or charming the director, no matter how worthy the nonprofit, will change their mind. Their decision comes from their heart and the hearts of three of their five children.

Jack explains why the bulk of their charitable giving is going to pediatric cardiology. It began, he says, with the birth of their third child and first son, Connor.

"We took him home from the hospital when he was two days old—our perfectly healthy boy, or so we thought. His big sisters were thrilled. We were cluelessly happy. On day five, Connor started to breathe oddly. Bet knew something wasn't right—he wasn't breastfeeding like the girls had."

When she called their pediatrician, he said he wasn't worried, but if it'd make them feel better, they could admit their newborn to the local hospital in Bronxville, N.Y., where they were living.

"A big shot cardiologist, or at least that was how he saw himself, came up from the city and pompously announced that it wasn't the baby's heart," Jack continued. "The next day Connor couldn't breathe. His one open heart valve had closed."

Their baby was immediately transported by helicopter to Cornell Medical Center in New York City, where the doctors said that his best chance was at Boston Children's Hospital. A second helicopter flew him from New York to Boston. Friends and relatives volunteered to take care of the couple's two daughters, so Jack and Bet could board the next flight to Boston. The extraordinary medical efforts were not successful. Connor died on the operating table.

"They let us in the room to hold him," said Jack. "It was as surreal as any moment in my life. I knew it was also the saddest moment. We had so much hope while he was enduring hours of surgery. Afterwards, with tears flowing and snow falling, we walked through a blizzard to collapse in our hotel room. I don't remember if we ate or slept. We were raw nerves.

"The next morning, reality hit. We had to get back to our daughters. We told them that Connor was in heaven and that we were sad, but we'd all be okay. I don't remember how they reacted.

"We were in a grief fog for a long time—maybe as long as two years—and, even today, we lapse into it. Grieving, working, taking care of our daughters, I felt that I had to be the rock for the family. I cried on long walks and in the shower. I shared my grief with my family and friends. I never got angry at God, but I questioned why **He let it happen**.

Because Jack is a numbers guy—he thought about the numbers and wondered if there was a chance that either of their daughters might have a heart problem.

Bet agreed that they should be checked out but said that she just couldn't go. Jack shared, "I took them myself. I am an optimist and was looking forward to giving Bet good news. It wasn't to be. I will never forget coming home from the doctor's visit. My daughters were playing on the swings in the back yard. I told Bet to brace herself. She leaned against the gym set as I told her that Caitlin needed surgery. She had a different heart problem than Connor but a significant one.

"I will never forget the horrific déjà vu of being back in the pediatric ICU at Cornell. The same sights, smells and sounds. The same fears.

"This time, the results were dramatically different. After being woozy for a few days, my post-op princess toddled down the hall pushing her little IV pole. She had a dressing on her back that covered half her tiny body. She had tubes coming out and needles going in, but she was emerging the same zippy kid that went into the hospital a few days before. Today, as an adult, she's still zippy, and I'm still recovering. Caitlin doesn't remember much. I can't forget much.

"As time passed, the trauma of heart surgery faded, and the stabbing pain of losing a child became a duller, persistent pain. Bet wanted another child, but I said I couldn't face it. I'd forgotten the part of the wedding vows where I was supposed to say, 'Yes dear.'"

Bet got pregnant with baby number four. For this pregnancy, the best place to get care was Yale, so the couple drove to Yale every other week for a sonogram. Each time the news was good: the baby's heart was developing normally.

"Even though we knew the situation was deadly serious," said Jack, "we tried to think of these day-long trips as outings and have some fun. We listened to different kinds of music on the drive. We explored new restaurants in New Haven. We tried to focus on the future."

Baby Liam was born with a dozen medical personnel in the delivery room—a high-risk OB, a pediatric cardiologist, a neonatologist and every other "ist" in the hospital—and without Connor's heart defect. With an 8.6 lb. baby in their arms and elation in their hearts, the couple headed home to introduce him to his sisters.

Nine months later, a pediatric cardiologist found that Liam had the same heart defect as his sister. Two weeks later, Jack and Bet and baby walked through the same doors at Boston Children's as they had walked into with Connor, the same doors they had walked out of without Connor. In the intervening years, surgical techniques had undergone radical changes, so instead of a 5" scar like his sister, Liam had four small incisions. He was crawling in no time.

"We decided no more kids," said Jack. "As Catholics, however, we understand the meaning of the phrase, 'Man plans, and God laughs.' Baby number five was on its way. This time was very different. We had a healthy baby, just like her oldest sister."

At this juncture in their family life, Jack received an offer he couldn't refuse and took a senior position in with a bank in St. Louis, as a senior VP in a major regional bank. One of the first things he did was join the board of the St. Louis Children's Hospital Foundation, where he served for 19 years. "I was honored to be asked."

I asked Jack why they didn't give to the hospitals where his children had been cared for. He had a simple answer: They never asked. St. Louis Children's asked.

Jack and Bet set the Connor Liam Stapleton Congenital Heart Fund as an endowed gift to St. Louis Children's. After being on the board of St. Louis Children's and meeting all the great scientists and physicians, they were encouraged by the great strides in pediatric cardiology. We got a front row seat at the remarkable work being done. "I sit in every board meeting and tear up when I hear about the incredible strides in multiple diseases."

Jack and Bet feel that their gifts of money are dwarfed by the gifts of time, talent and love. We visit with families dealing with our challenges. We get to work with the young medical professionals to share what it is like for a family. We raise funds for additional research.

When asked about his philosophy of giving, he said that he got it from his father, who transformed street smarts growing up one of nine in the Bronx into a successful banking career. "When I was little, I would watch my dad "desking," and ask him what he was doing. He said that he was paying bills and writing checks to charity. He gave monthly gifts to our parish, our schools and Boy's Town of Nebraska. My mother gave differently. She made sure that people in the neighborhood and the parish got what they needed. Her approach to giving was upfront and personal. She did the vetting herself rather than through large institutions."

Fifteen years after Jack's mother died, his father was on his deathbed when he made an enormous donation to Fordham University. He had been a major fan of the basketball team and the Jesuits. A locker room on the campus is named after him. I asked Jack how he felt about so much of what would have been his inheritance going elsewhere. "Dad had already been generous with us kids," said Jack, "and it wasn't my money. The gift made my dad very happy."

Like his father, Jack shares an interest in education and gives money to support his high school, his college, and several inner-city school programs. "I believe in faith-based education," he said. "I want inner-city kids to have the same opportunities as my children." He gives to education in his lifetime, but not in his will.

What is most impressive about Jack is his *joie de vivre*. "I can live with an open and charitable heart," he said, "because I've already experienced the worst day of my life."

Lessons learned

For nonprofit professionals and leaders: Some people have defining events in their lives that determine their first, largest and most passionate gift. They may well give to you but accept their priority and be content with second place.

On the other hand, what appears to be a priority may not always be the case. Years ago, a livid executive director called me with a question. "My board president, who donates $5,000 a year to us, is being honored by another charity for donating $5 million, and he wants me to sit at his table. Do I have to go?" I answered, "Unless you can be gracious, no. It would, however, be a good opportunity to learn more about the gift. Why don't you ask the man why he gave $5,000 to your charity and $5 million to the other?" The executive director followed my advice. His board president responded: "If you come up with a $5 million idea, I'm open to matching the amount I'm giving to my other charity." The executive started to think bigger. Go ahead and ask. The worst that can happen is that someone says no.

For some donors, like Jack and Bet, pediatric cardiology will always be first and foremost. Ask, then accept and respect their choice.

For donors: If you have a major philanthropic theme in your family, such as a commitment to your place of worship, a familial disease, or a history of military service, think through what you would have done if your life had been different and be open to other opportunities to give time and money. Prioritize what is important for the next generation. It's meaningful and gratifying to give the bulk of your charitable dollars to something dear to your heart in this life and the next. But also consider giving an unrestricted gift. The reason being is that research might make the heart defects a thing of the past. The change between Jack's daughter's surgery and his sons was the difference between a five-inch scar and four little quarter-inch scars. They might want to consider giving to pediatric cardiac research, rather than to finding a cure for a specific heart defect.

I know this is difficult for people who like control. If that is you, give more in your lifetime. But if you wrote a will, let's say in 1980. There was no HIV that we knew of, there were no solar panels, women didn't have a combat role in the military. This is why giving unrestricted makes so much more sense. You have to let go and trust the future leadership.

A quiet evening at the Robbins-Weisman household.

— 13 —

"Too Bad, So Sad, Be On Time"
Carol Weisman

When our son Jono was 18, we told him that he and his brother had to come with us to the lawyer's office to discuss our will.

"No," he said, "it's ghoulish."

"May I remind you that when you were 16, you made funeral urns in your ceramics class and gave them to us for Christmas. You don't have a leg to stand on."

They went with us to the lawyer's office. As we have changed our will over the years, they continue to attend these meetings. When they lived in other cities, we consulted them by phone. They never wanted to be part of this conversation. Being the kind and sympathetic mother that I am, I always said, "Too bad. So sad. Be on time."

We have always consulted our children on major life decisions. When they were five and seven, we asked them who they wanted to live with if something were to happen to us. Like many people who travel abroad without their children, we believed this question needed to be answered and, in fact, was long overdue. Frank and I come from large families. I am the oldest of four and Frank, the fourth of seven. Our children had never met four of Frank's siblings; two of mine lived out of town, one was single. Grandparents were not an option because of age, illness or death.

The kids chose our friends Pat and Mike Wolff.

"Whose kids will we get if their parents die?" asked Jono.

I named eleven.

Jono burst into tears. "We don't have room for all of these kids!" he said.

"It's highly unlikely that we will get even one, much less eleven," I reassured him.

A skeptical child, he wrapped his arms around his little body, dipped his chin and gave me the stink eye.

During our discussion of custody issues, the boys were stunned to learn that a parent could die. It never occurred to them. They had no friends or cousins who had lost a parent, and here we were talking about both of us passing away.

"Okay," Jono finally relented. "I'll move in with another family as long as I can take my friend Chad."

Another long discussion ensued.

In case Frank and I died at the same time, we also wrote Pat and Mike a detailed letter. In it we shared our philosophy of parenting and our desires for our children. We had taken out a large life insurance policy on Frank, because when the kids were little, I wasn't working outside the home and I'm not that cute, so I figured a sizable policy was a good idea. This was the era of Bo Derek, the quintessential 10. I figured with a ton of life insurance I could rocket from a five to an eight. And this rationale coming from someone who considered herself a feminist! Anyway, if we both died at once, the Wolffs could use the life insurance money to spend traveling the world with our children and theirs. We specified that the Wolffs pay for our sons to visit their out-of-town grandparents at least twice a year or to pay for the grandparents to come to St. Louis. And if the Wolff family wanted a larger house, we wanted them to feel free to use the money for that as well. College wasn't an issue, because tuition would be covered by Washington University, where Frank taught. Because of this benefit, we suggested that the Wolffs not adopt our kids. We expressed our deep gratitude for their willingness to take on this enormous responsibility. And finally, we thanked Pat and Mike, and their sons Ben and Andy, for making room in their lives and in their hearts for our sons. Fortunately, the letter never had to be opened.

Frank and I knew to pay attention to these matters, because both our families had experienced estate-planning folly. When my mother was dying, she confessed an incident that had weighed on her. When my father's Uncle Julius became extremely ill, Julius asked my mother to take him to a lawyer because he didn't have a will. My physician mom took one look at his labored breathing and decided to take him to the hospital first. A few hours later, Uncle Julius died in the ER.

His death might have been blessedly quick, but the legal aftermath was torturous. Relatives emerged from the proverbial woodwork. Uncle Julius spent most of his time visiting his sister who lived with her daughter, my Aunt Ruth. (I am afraid you almost need a chart for this!) Aunt Ruth always had room for one more at the table. In fact, had the entire Vienna Boys Choir dropped by, she would have embraced them, urged them to sing, and then fed them. Aunt Ruth was a life grandmaster at bridge, a home cook who could whip up world-class fudge in eight minutes, and a cheerleader who always told me how pretty I looked, even when I had acne. She and her husband did not have much money, and if Uncle Julius had written a will, she would have inherited his estate. And she should have. She cared for Uncle Julius for years with kindness and humor. Ultimately, she gave up the fight and let the vultures ransack the carcass of his estate. Mom felt so guilty and ashamed that she hadn't honored Uncle Julius's wishes and taken him to a lawyer that she never revealed this story to my father. She told it to me two days before she died.

Frank's family has a different story but a similar theme. His great aunt, Auntie Ann, had never married or had children and lived in an old Victorian house in San

Francisco. Her neighbors poured hundreds of thousands of dollars into their homes in the 1960s and 1970s. When these houses sold, their sale prices were public knowledge. Auntie Ann assumed the value of her house—her only asset—had risen as sky-high as the tarted-up houses around her. But she had not updated the kitchen or painted a wall since she moved in shortly after World War II. We are talking the days of avocado-green kitchens and crimson-flocked wallpaper. Plus, her house was smaller and simpler than those around her. When Auntie Ann died in the late 1970s, she left $150,000 to each of five large charities. The house sold for $450,000. You don't have to be a math whiz to realize that the numbers didn't gel.

My father-in-law, a patent attorney as well as Auntie Ann's nephew, was the executor. The charities came after him with a vengeance. They assumed he had sold the property to a friend and pocketed the profits. The facts were very different. He was a highly ethical man who took his commitment as an officer of the court seriously. But neither estate planning nor real estate law was his field of expertise. Plus, he had been a longtime donor to four of the five charities, a generosity the charities considered irrelevant. They were out for blood and consumed two years of his life to drain it. Auntie Ann had made another false assumption: That because her nephew was a lawyer he was loaded. In fact, he had seven kids, six of whom were in college at the same time. He could have well used a bequest.

Frank and I benefited from the debacles our families experienced with estate planning. We wanted our loved ones and the charities we cared about to mourn if they felt like it but, more importantly, to joyously spend our money to make lives better.

That is why we decided early on to have candid (only because the word "frank" is used so often as a name in our family) conversations with our children and include them in the decision making. These conversations are not easy, but we believe they are important. We always reviewed our estate plans before traveling outside the country without the kids. In hindsight, it was a ridiculous criterion. We were not mountain climbers or race car drivers or paragliders. We did very little espionage work in back alleys. We were going to conferences in Edinburgh, Munich and London. We should have reviewed our wills every time we rode in a car together, since statistically it's more dangerous to drive than to fly. I never said we were rational! Few people are. A dear friend had a fit when we took our kids to Egypt. We were just asking for trouble, she said. Meanwhile, she and her then three-year-old son were held up by a serial killer named Michael Wayne Jackson on the parking lot of an upscale mall in St. Louis. What can I say?

There were times when our sons were glad that they had attended the meetings with the attorney. At one such meeting, we were leaving funds to the high school where our son Jono teaches ceramics. He called the next day to ask if we had specified the art department. We hadn't, so we called the attorney to make the change—crisis averted. At the same meeting, we asked the boys if they wanted to be co-executors. Our son Jono said not a chance; our other son agreed to take on the task. I pointed out that the executor would be paid. Jono didn't care. We asked if they were both good with this arrangement, and they both said yes.

Frank and I share a philosophy of generosity both to our families and to those in need outside our families. This philosophy was modeled to us by both sets of parents. My mother, widowed at 52, was well off and enjoyed giving us money. We loved having it. She helped all four of us—I have two sisters and a brother—buy our first homes. She paid for all our undergrad and grad school educations. My siblings and I all went into helping professions. One sister is a retired ob-gyn, one is a nurse and my brother and I are social workers. None of us grew up to become entitled, bratty adults. (Others might disagree, but they can write their own book!)

There was only one time my mother had to bite her tongue. Decades ago, she had given each of us $1,000. She wanted my sister to buy a washer-dryer rather than have to schlep to the laundromat. My sister and her husband put the money into savings instead. Mom wasn't happy, but she demonstrated amazing grace and said nothing. Once the funds left her account, she believed that we could do with them what we wanted. They weren't a loan; they were a gift.

We appreciated my mother's generosity so we, in turn, have helped our children buy their first homes.

Frank's parents were also generous, but with seven kids and a smaller income than my parents had, it wasn't possible for them to give as much. But their generosity came in the form of time as well as money. They lived across the highway from us when our kids were little. Had it not been for them, we never would have had Saturday date nights or 24-hour-a-day support when we most needed it.

As our lives continue to evolve, so has our will. We have removed people from our bequests because of changes in relationships, and we have removed organizations because of changes in mission or leadership. One local chapter of a national organization sent us a note saying that they had matching funds and would like to know how much we were leaving the chapter. I had never talked to anyone in the development department, had never met the person who signed the letter, which requested a copy of our will and a dollar amount. I later discovered that a friend on the board mentioned to the development director that this organization was in our will. The development director must have recorded this information in the database. I called the executive director and left a voice message: "I am dumbfounded by the note I received from your organization and don't understand where the money is going, who is donating the matching funds, or any of the details." The letter sounded as though they thought I was an ATM and wanted only a balance receipt. The executive director called back, but I missed the call. After I left a second message, I didn't hear from her for three weeks. That's lousy stewardship. When she finally did call, she explained that there was another piece of paper that should have been enclosed with the letter. No apology for the three-week delay, no offer to have coffee. We dropped this chapter as a beneficiary, but because we still believe in its mission we made the bequest instead to the national organization.

We dropped another charity from our will that rebranded so many times, today I don't even know its name. I was once a devoted and generous board member. Too bad, so sad, goodbye.

On the other hand, there have been organizations that have wowed us with their leadership, mission and outcomes. Welcome to the fold. One group that we cherish hired a new leader who was both charismatic and knowledgeable about programming and fundraising. He turned the ship around, and we put it in our estate.

Currently our estate is divided so that each son gets 40%. Other people we care about get 10%. Only one person gets a specific amount. That's John Russell, our friend, neighbor and wealth advisor. We left him $1,000 to take a friend to dinner and the theater in New York. Since we wrote this pre-"Hamilton," leaving a specific amount was a mistake we'll have to correct. If we don't change it and live another 20 years, the $1,000 might enable John to ride a Greyhound bus to New York—alone—dine at Shake Shack and take in a puppet show in Queens. The final 10% goes to charity. Four charities get 20% of that and the final 20% of the charitable portion is to be decided by our grandchildren.

If our younger son, currently single, gets married and has kids, we may change our will to include the next generation. As it is now, we want to avoid leaving money to one batch of grandchildren, while the next crew gets nothing because they were born after we died.

We have no idea what our estate will be worth by the time we die. We could be hit by a car driven by a wealthy alcoholic. We could watch our stocks crash or soar. We could suffer long illnesses that soak up every penny. Because of these variables we have left everything in percentages.

If I die first, I have asked Frank to promise that he will date for at least six weeks before getting remarried. Our courtship lasted only three weeks, so I want him to have some fun. This is not in the estate plan, but if I have departed this good earth and you know Frank, make sure he doesn't run off with someone at my funeral!

Lessons learned

For board and staff in the nonprofit field: You need to continue to steward your donors. Treat all donors as though they have made revocable gifts. Our gifts are all revocable, and people do change their wills. The more you know the entire family, the more likely a family member will not contest a donation. The more likely, too, that you will cultivate a second generation of donors. Ask donors if they would like to bring their children to see how their parents are changing the world.

For donors with children: Consider including your children in your decision-making. Spell out where and with whom your minor children will live if you both die at the same time. There will be no opportunity to explain decisions after you are gone.

Share your thoughts and reasons for leaving different amounts to different children. A mantra of children everywhere is "No fair." I don't know about your family, but my mother always said, "This is an unfair world." I remember my first experience with the green-eyed monster of envy.

My sister Nancy got to have glasses when she was three. They had to be trifocals because Nancy was already reading. My mother, in a moment of madness, let my father go with Nancy to pick out the frames. In 1953, they cost over $100. My father's philosophy was that if she liked them, she would wear them more. The frames had to be made from scratch. Nancy chose a cat's eye pair with multi-colored glitter. I couldn't have been more envious. My mother was appalled.

At age five, I had an appendectomy and found out that you get far more loot when something is removed than when a fashion/reading device is acquired.

The bottom line, it isn't a fair world. Through our philanthropy, we can give people a hand, we can preserve and create art forms we love, we can help make the environment a better place for everyone ... and the list goes on. Pick whatever makes sense to you and give generously.

Giving Questionnaire

1. Why do you want to give? (check all that apply)
___To make a difference or give back
___To honor or memorialize a friend, mentor, or loved one
___To express gratitude
___To express religious/spiritual conviction
___To feel good about helping less fortunate
___To fight a disease or misfortune
___To reduce taxes
___To support my community or favorite community institutions
___To support issues or causes important to my friends or loved ones
___To leave a legacy
___Other reason: _____

_____

2. Your philanthropic interests:
A) What types of causes are important to you? (rank in order #1 most etc.)
___Basic needs such as food, clean water, housing
___Safety, caring, and stability for children
___Provide solutions to community dangers/ problems/ deficiencies

___Rescue groups for dogs/cats/horses/other

___Social justice/racism/sexism, etc.

___Faith/spiritual/place of worship

___Immigrants/refugees/displaced people

___Cure and care for a specific disease or condition

___Educational: institution that you or a loved one attended or to offer an opportunity for self sufficiency

___Health: prevention and maintenance, physical/ mental

___Music, arts & culture

___Nature/parks/environment protection/species retention

B. What good works do you value most?

What are you most passionate about? _____

_____

What makes you angry? _____

_____

What breaks your heart?_____

_____

What is your family's history of helping? _____

_____

_____

3. What kind of legacy do you want to leave?_____

_____

_____

_____

4. What or who influences your decision as to which charities to support? (check all that apply)

___Charity size or number of charities

___Geographic location

___Family

___Friends

___Experiences

___Others

___Trusted advisors: CPA, attorney, financial advisor, spiritual leader

5. How often and when do you want to give?

___Every month or every year

___When you're sure you have enough retirement income

___When you've reached a specific goal such as paying off loans, college, wedding, etc.

___After you die

___Some now, some later

6. How much do you want to give?

___5-10% of your income (gross or net)? Or another percent? ____ %

___$xxxx (specific annual goal for financial support)

___Do you have a budgeted time based amount in mind (Y/N), it is $_____ over __ years or __over my lifetime.

7. How active do you want to be with your giving? (check all that apply)

___Provide episodic volunteer time

___Provide regular volunteer talent (website/social media/PR/engineering/fixing or renovating charity's building, plantings, or extending other skills to help the organization)

___Working as a board or trustee or committee member

___Donate cash, gifts in kind, or other investments

___Combination of above

Reprinted with permission from
Nina Needleman, nina_needl@yahoo.com

Acknowledgments

Ever hear the joke, "A lawyer, a doctor and an engineer walk into a bar and start discussing their estate plans?"

No? Probably because there is no such joke, as the majority of people don't have an estate plan. Figures vary, but most studies find that around 65% of Americans don't have a will, trust or estate plan. One reason is that many people are uncomfortable discussing their death or life afterwards. People may talk about sex, politics, and money in general but not how they plan to dispose of their possessions and their money. It is the taboo of taboo subjects.

My greatest thanks go to the people who shared their stories. They confided their pains, losses, joys, and hopes for the future. Their interviews took courage. They are my heroes.

This book would not have been possible without the help and guidance of my editors, Cheryl Jarvis and Brian Jarvis, and my graphic design pro, Peggy Nehmen. A very special thank to Catherine Bakewell, eagle-eye editor.

As always, thanks to my always-supportive husband, Frank Robbins. He brought me endless cups of coffee, held me when I was frustrated and listened to me rant when the process slowed. (I am not actually sure he listened, but he shook his head from time to time, which worked for me.)

A very special thanks to my sons Frank V and Jono Robbins and my daughter-in-law Laura. Were it not for them, I would be the Widow Weisman. I went to work in Akron, Ohio, on a day that my husband, Frank IV, wasn't feeling well. I asked our son Frank V to check on him. He ran by in the morning and later brought him lunch. Our other son, Jono, came by in the late afternoon. Laura suggested that her husband spend the night. Frank V threw some beers in the car and expected to watch some testosterone-laden TV with his dad. Instead, he found him in septic shock on the floor, where he had been lying for hours. After surgery and a slew of antibiotics, Frank IV is back biking in the park and observing his birdie buddies. And finally, my grandsons, Frank VI (do you see a trend?), Tommy and Eli. Their observations about the world, their dancing and the tricks they play on their parents keep my heart filled with joy and my belly laughing.

It isn't over till it's over!
Jerry Horwitz age 83

Thank you for reading this book ...

If you are looking for a motivational keynote, a facilitator for a retreat or a workshop on how to ask for a major, capital or planned gift or just need to get your board to understand their roles and responsibilities, please call me at 314-863-4422, e-mail me at Carol@BoardBuilders.com or check out my website www.BoardBuilders.com.

Raising Charitable Children, based on my book by the same name, is also a popular topic. This topic has been particularly popular with community foundations, the clients of wealth advisors, places of worship and schools. What makes me unique? I believe I am the only fundraising speaker who has also done stand-up comedy. I can also tap dance ... badly, but I keep taking lessons. If AARP revises "A Chorus Line," I will be ready.

If you are interested in bulk sales of 10 copies or more of any of my books for your entire team or donors, please contact Board Builders directly.

And finally, this book is outdated the day it goes to press. The laws changed dramatically while writing this tomb and they will continue to change. If there are changes that you are aware of, please let me know and I can incorporate them immediately in the downloadable version.

I hope this book gave you a path forward in leaving a legacy that you are proud of.

Fondly,
Carol